CONSECRATION TO
ST. JOSEPH
for Children and Families

Scott L. Smith, Jr.
and **Donald H. Calloway, MIC**

D1248578

Available from:
Marian Helpers Center, Stockbridge, MA 01263

Prayerline: 1-800-804-3823
Orderline: 1-800-462-7426
Websites: fathercalloway.com
consecrationtostjoseph.org

Publication Date:
May 1, 2022
Feast of St. Joseph the Worker

Imprimi Potest
Very Rev. Kazimierz Chwalek, MIC
Provincial Superior
The Blessed Virgin Mary, Mother of Mercy Province
March 19, 2022
Solemnity of St. Joseph

Nihil Obstat
Robert A. Stackpole, STD
Censor Deputatus
March 19, 2022

Note: The *Nihil Obstat* and corresponding *Imprimatur* and/or
Imprimi Potest is not a certification that those granting it agree with
the contents, opinions, or statements expressed in the work; instead, it
merely confirms that it contains nothing contrary to faith or morals.

ISBN: 978-1-59614-564-1

Design by Curtis Bohner

Cover Image: The artist of the cover image is unknown. All attempts have
been made by Marian Press to locate and give credit to the artist. In the
event that the identity of the artist becomes known, all due recognition
will be given in future editions.

Printed in the United States of America

MARIAN PRESS
STOCKBRIDGE MA 01263

To my wife Ashton and our children — Lucy, Charlie, Elijah, Elizabeth, Jude Bosco and all our future children — who have sat around the dinner table with me to consecrate themselves to Jesus, Mary, and Joseph.

— Scott L. Smith, Jr.

In thanksgiving to the Holy Trinity for unveiling the greatness of St. Joseph in our times.

— Fr. Donald H. Calloway, MIC

Table of Contents

INTRODUCTION

by Scott L. Smith, Jr.

Go to Joseph, the mender of broken toys,
furniture, houses, as well as broken hearts, souls,
bodies, minds, and families. Yes, let us go to
Joseph, whom Jesus and Mary love so much.[1]

– Servant of God Catherine Doherty

This *Consecration to St. Joseph for Children and Families* is modeled very closely after the one created by Fr. Donald Calloway, MIC. Father Calloway has also shepherded this consecration along every step of the way.

Believing "the world needs St. Joseph now more than ever," Fr. Calloway created a *Consecration of St. Joseph* and published a book of the same title in 2020. Father Calloway's consecration to St. Joseph is modeled after the consecration to Mary of St. Louis de Montfort.

Father Calloway has stated that "the first person to entrust himself to the spiritual care of Joseph and Mary was actually Jesus." In his book, Fr. Calloway writes that consecration to St. Joseph means "that you acknowledge that he is your spiritual father, and you want to be like him. To show it, you entrust yourself entirely to his paternal care so that he can lovingly help you acquire his virtues and become holy. St. Joseph, in turn, will give those consecrated to him his loving attention, protection and guidance."

Father Calloway's book *Consecration to St. Joseph: The Wonders of Our Spiritual Father* has sold more than one million copies worldwide and is available in over nineteen languages. A website is maintained for the book at www.consecrationtostjoseph.org.

Overview of
Consecration to St. Joseph

by Scott L. Smith, Jr.

A re you looking at your calendar? This Consecration to St. Joseph will last 33 total days.

The next 33 days of prayers and readings are preparation for your and your children's *Act of Consecration to St. Joseph*. You will make your consecration on Day 33.

You will start to notice that Fr. Calloway organized the days of the Consecration to St. Joseph to follow the Litany of St. Joseph. Each line of the Litany of St. Joseph is expanded into a day of the consecration.

Don't just read the readings, internalize them. Don't let your lips just mouth the prayers and the readings; truly pray them. Just saying the words won't work; it's not a magic incantation.

You may feel less motivated or less focused some days, but persevere. You may even miss a day. Keep going. Keep trying.

How Do I Do This With My Family?

Ultimately, that's up to you. I will tell you how my wife and I do these consecrations with our family.

I will tell you right off that it's not always easy, but it is always fruitful. Incredibly fruitful.

My wife and I do this consecration as a lead up to Christmas. We use it as an Advent exercise to help our family focus on Jesus' coming and birth.

We repeat the consecration every year, too. So don't worry if your kids aren't understanding everything this year. You're building towards next year. And the next year.

We do this with the whole family around the dinner table. Even the very young ones, like those still in a high chair. I will tell you that my copies of our family consecrations are stained with food, because *yes!* the kids can lose focus. Peas very likely will fly between me and the book at some point.

There are ways to help with short attention spans. I have tried to pepper this book with lots of questions and illustrations to engage the kids (and let's face it, we parents need it, too).

Feel free to add in your own discussion questions, too — this is the Socratic method of learning. Also, feel free to read ahead and summarize the readings with your kids.

Always remember that your kids are learning about the Holy Family no matter what it may seem like. The Holy Spirit *will* come to your aid.

Also remember that, we don't fail our kids when we lose their undivided attention. We only fail our kids by expecting too little from them. Every child has a future hero-saint inside them.

Picking a Start Date

If you can, you want to plan your consecration so it ends on one of St. Joseph's feast days. We have provided a handy table of possible start dates below.

Here are St. Joseph's feast days and possible start dates for your Consecration to St. Joseph, i.e., the dates that fall 33 days before the feast day:

START OF THE 33 DAYS	FEAST DAY	CONSECRATION DAY
December 22	Feast of the Holy Spouses	January 23
January 1	Presentation of the Lord	February 2
February 15*	Solemnity of St. Joseph	March 19
March 30	St. Joseph the Worker	May 1
April 11	Our Lady of Fatima	May 13
July 16	Our Lady of Knock	August 17
September 30	All Saints	November 1
November 8	Our Lady of Loreto	December 10
November**	Holy Family	December

* During a leap year, when February has 29 days, the starting date is February 16.

** The Solemnity of the Holy Family generally falls on the First Sunday after Christmas. If Christmas itself is on a Sunday, be sure to check what day the bishops designate as the Solemnity of the Holy Family and begin your consecration 32 days before the consecration date (Day 33).

Overview of the Consecration

The 33 days of this Consecration are divided into different sections, each with its own prayers to complement the daily readings. The Litany of St. Joseph will be prayed every day as well. This is how the days will be divided:

Days 1-7: Why Consecrate to St. Joseph?

First comes an overview of salvation history and how St. Joseph fits into all this. You will start your journey in the Garden with Adam and Eve. You will then journey, through time, to the New Garden, the home of the New Adam, Jesus, and the New Eve, Mary. We will learn to entrust our families to St. Joseph to keep them holy, because God, Himself, entrusted the Holy Family to St. Joseph.

Days 8-15: The Life of St. Joseph

Who was St. Joseph? Days 8-15 focus on what the Bible tells us about St. Joseph: the angel visiting St. Joseph in his dreams, the journey to Bethlehem, the journey to Egypt, and the hidden years he spent with Jesus and Mary in Nazareth.

Days 16-22: Saint Joseph, Increaser of Virtues

Days 16-22 focus on the virtues. What are the virtues? What are the vices and how do we defeat them with virtue? How can St. Joseph increase the virtues – justice, chastity, prudence, courage, obedience, faithfulness, and patience – in us?

Days 23-33: Saint Joseph, Minister of Salvation

Days 23-33 focus on how St. Joseph is still active in the world. In the final days before your consecration, we seek to better understand how St. Joseph will protect our families and teach us to be better Christians. You will spend these days in the humble home of Nazareth. Saint Joseph will open the door of his home to you, so you can spend your life, as he did, in the arms of Jesus and Mary.

Consecration Day

Frequently Asked Questions

Can I Just Start Now?
Do I have to Wait for a St. Joseph Feast Day?

There's no time like the present. Your children's attention is a precious resource. If they want to start now, go ahead.

It is customary to re-consecrate yourself every year on the same date. That's part of the reason you are advised to look ahead and choose a special date, especially a special St. Joseph date.

If you miss the St. Joseph feast day this year, maybe plan it out for next year.

Do Parents Need to be Consecrated First?

Do you need to be consecrated to St. Joseph (or to Mary) before you can lead your children in a consecration?

No. Let *this* be your first consecration, if you haven't done one before.

My wife and I like to pray our consecrations together. Husbands and wives that pray together, stay together. The structure of a consecration is a great means to enhance or begin your marital prayer habit.

PRAYERS

The Litany of St. Joseph

Lord, have mercy.   *Lord, have mercy.*

Christ, have mercy.   *Christ, have mercy.*

Lord, have mercy.   *Lord, have mercy.*

Christ, hear us.   *Christ, graciously hear us.*

God, the Father of Heaven,	*have mercy on us.*
God the Son, Redeemer of the world,	*have mercy on us.*
God the Holy Spirit,	*have mercy on us.*
Holy Trinity, One God,	*have mercy on us.*

Holy Mary,	*pray for us.*
Saint Joseph,	*pray for us.*
Noble Offspring of David,	*pray for us.*
Light of Patriarchs,	*pray for us.*
Spouse of the Mother of God,	*pray for us.*
Guardian of the Redeemer,	*pray for us.*
Chaste Guardian of the Virgin,	*pray for us.*
Foster-Father of the Son of God,	*pray for us.*
Zealous Defender of Christ,	*pray for us.*
Servant of Christ,	*pray for us.*
Minister of Salvation,	*pray for us.*
Head of the Holy Family,	*pray for us.*

Joseph Most Just,	*pray for us.*
Joseph Most Chaste,	*pray for us.*
Joseph Most Prudent,	*pray for us.*
Joseph Most Courageous,	*pray for us.*
Joseph Most Obedient,	*pray for us.*
Joseph Most Faithful,	*pray for us.*

Mirror of Patience,	*pray for us.*
Lover of Poverty,	*pray for us.*
Model of Workmen,	*pray for us.*
Glory of Domestic Life,	*pray for us.*
Guardian of Virgins,	*pray for us.*

Pillar of Families,	*pray for us.*
Support in Difficulties,	*pray for us.*
Comfort of the Afflicted,	*pray for us.*
Hope of the Sick,	*pray for us.*
Patron of Exiles,	*pray for us.*
Patron of the Afflicted,	*pray for us.*
Patron of the Poor,	*pray for us.*
Patron of the Dying,	*pray for us.*
Terror of Demons,	*pray for us.*
Protector of the Holy Church,	*pray for us.*

Lamb of God, who takes away the sins of the world,
                              Spare us, O Lord.

Lamb of God, who takes away the sins of the world,
                         Graciously hear us, O Lord.

Lamb of God, who takes away the sins of the world,
                              Have mercy on us.

V. He has made him lord of his household,

R. And prince over all his possessions.

Let us pray. *O God, who, in your loving providence, chose Blessed Joseph to be the spouse of your most Holy Mother, grant us the favor of having him for our intercessor in heaven whom on earth we venerate as our protector. You, who live and reign forever and ever. Amen.*

The "Our Father"

Our Father who art in heaven,
hallowed be thy name;
thy kingdom come.
thy will be done
on earth, as it is in heaven.
Give us this day our daily bread,
and forgive us our trespasses,

as we forgive those who trespass against us;
and lead us not into temptation,
but deliver us from evil.
Amen.

The "Hail Mary"

Hail Mary, full of grace, the Lord is with thee.
Blessed art thou among women and
blessed is the fruit of thy womb, Jesus.
Holy Mary, Mother of God, pray for us sinners,
now and at the hour of our death.
Amen.

The Prayer of Blessed Bartolo Longo to St. Joseph

Prostrate at your feet, O great saint, I venerate you as the father of my Lord and my God. You are the Head of the Holy Family, and a cause of joy and delight to the Holy Trinity.

What a glory for you to be the father of a Son who is God's Only Begotten Son! What a blessing to know that you are a father to us and that we are your children. Yes, we are your children because we are brothers and sisters of Jesus Christ, who wanted to be called your Son.

As your children, we have a right to the tenderness and goodness of your fatherly heart. Accept us and take us under your protection! Teach us to love patience, prudence, kindness, modesty, and purity. Be our safe place and hope in all our pains, in all our needs, both now and at the hour of our death. Amen.

Prayer of Pope St. Pius X[1]

O Joseph, virgin father of Jesus, most pure spouse of the Virgin Mary, pray for us daily to the same Jesus, the Son of God that, armed with the weapons of his grace, we may fight as we ought during life, and be crowned by him at the moment of our death. Amen.

Children's Memorare Prayer to St. Joseph

Please remember to help me, St. Joseph.

St. Joseph, you are the most chaste spouse of the Virgin Mary.

St. Joseph, you always help people who ask for your help.

St. Joseph, I am confident that you can help me.

St. Joseph, I come before you. I hold your strong carpenter's hands. I beg you for your help and protection.

St. Joseph, please do not refuse my humble request. Because you are so good and so strong, please listen to my prayers and answer my prayers.

Amen.

Traditional Memorare Prayer to St. Joseph

Remember, O most chaste spouse of the Virgin Mary, that never was it known that anyone who implored your help and sought your intercession were left unaided.

Full of confidence in your power I fly to you and beg your protection.

Despise not, O Guardian of the Redeemer my humble supplication, but in your bounty, hear and answer me. Amen.

Prayer Taught to the Children at Fatima

Repeat 3 Times

My God, I believe, I adore, I hope, and I love you.

I ask pardon for those who do not believe, nor adore, nor hope, nor love you.

Children's Act of Consecration to St. Joseph

I, [state your name], a child of God, take you, St. Joseph, to be my spiritual father. I know that Jesus and Mary have brought me to you. Jesus and Mary want me to know you, to love you, and to be totally consecrated to you, St. Joseph, my father forever.

I have spent many days coming to know and love you better. Now, I consecrate myself to you, St. Joseph. I want you in my life more and more. I need you in my life. Take me as your spiritual child, O great St. Joseph! Please take all that I am and give it to Jesus. I do not want to hold anything back.

As the husband of Mary, you provided for my spiritual mother. Thank you for always being faithful to her. Thank you for loving her. Thank you for giving your entire life to serving Mary and Jesus.

As the virginal father of Jesus, you cared for my Lord. You protected my Lord from evil men. Thank you for guarding the life of my Savior. Thanks to you, Jesus was able to sacrifice His life for me on the Cross. Thanks to you, St. Joseph, I can hope for everlasting life in Heaven.

As my spiritual father, I trust that you will guide and protect me, as you guided and protected Jesus and Mary. Please increase in me virtues and holiness and prayerfulness. I want to grow to be more and more like you, St. Joseph. I want to be pure, humble, loving, and merciful, like you.

Now that I am yours and you are mine, I promise never to forget you. I know you will never forget me. This gives me such great joy! I am loved by St. Joseph! I belong forever to St. Joseph!

Praise to the Holy Trinity – the Father, the Son, and the Holy Spirit – who has blessed you and raised you to be the greatest saint after the Virgin Mary.

Praise also to the Virgin Mary, who loves you and wants all the world to love you.

Praise to you, St. Joseph, my father, my guardian, my all! Amen.

Family Act of Consecration to St. Joseph

We, the _____ family, take you, St. Joseph, to be our spiritual father. We are confident that Jesus and Mary have led us to you; to know you, to love you, and to be totally consecrated to you.

Therefore, having come to know and love you, we consecrate our family entirely to you, St. Joseph. We want you in our lives; we need you in our lives. Take us as your spiritual children, O great St. Joseph! We desire to hold nothing back from your protective fatherhood.

As the husband of Mary, you provided for our spiritual mother. Thank you for always being faithful to her. Thank you for loving her and giving your entire life for her service.

As the virginal father of Jesus, you cared for our Lord and protected Him from evil men. Thank you for guarding the life of our Savior. Thanks to you, Jesus was able to shed His Blood for us on the Cross. Thanks to you, St. Joseph, we have hope of everlasting life in Heaven.

As our spiritual father, we know that you will guide and protect us, too. Please instruct us in the ways of prayer, virtue, and holiness. We want to be like you, St. Joseph. We want to be pure, humble, loving, and merciful.

Now that we are yours and you are ours, we promise never to forget you. We know that you will never forget us, and this gives us boundless joy! We are loved by St. Joseph! We belong to St. Joseph! Amen!

DAYS 1-7: OVERVIEW

Why Consecrate to St. Joseph?

Do you remember what happened to Adam and Eve, our first parents? God made the earth, the Sun, and the planets, the plants and animals, and the first family. God also gave the first family rules and laws.

All families have rules. What are the rules of your family? Are you allowed to make messes? Or are you supposed to clean up after yourself? What happens if everybody keeps making messes and nobody cleans up? A big, BIG mess!

Usually, mom and dad will help clean up the mess if it gets too big, right? When mom and dad are done helping you clean, your room should be spotless – even "immaculate."

But what if mom and dad make the mess?

Adam and Eve made a big mess. A BIG mess. Adam and Eve's mess was so big that it affected the whole world. Adam and Eve's mess is still messing up the world. This is what we call Original Sin.

Again, what if mom and dad make the mess? Will mom and dad's mom and dad clean up their mess? Uh-oh. Adam and Eve didn't have parents.

They had God – thank God! Adam and Eve's mess was so big that only God could fix it.

So how did God fix Adam and Eve's mess?

As soon as Adam and Eve messed up, God was ready to clean up their mess. But it would take time. A long time.

As soon as Adam and Eve messed up, God pointed to a future woman.[1] God said, I will make a woman who is pure and sinless. She will be the Immaculate Conception. This future woman will be a Virgin and will bear My Son.

God knew this pure woman and baby would be in danger. Adam and Eve's mess would make the world a deadly and dangerous place.

God knew the Virgin and her baby would need a protector. God knew He was sending these perfect lambs into a world of wolves. The Virgin and her baby would need a shepherd, bravely wielding his shepherd's staff, to scare and drive away wolves and other predators.

God entrusted the Virgin Mary and her baby – the Holy Family – to St. Joseph to keep them safe.

So, we will entrust our families to St. Joseph, as God did, to keep our families safe and holy.

Consecrated to St. Joseph, we will keep our family pure and free of messes. Under St. Joseph's protection, the light of the world, Jesus, will shine in our families. And through our families, the light of Jesus will illuminate the whole world.

DAY 1

St. Joseph, "The Increaser"

Do you know what St. Joseph's name means? "Joseph" means "Increase." St. Joseph is the "Increaser."

The Increaser! Does that sound like a Marvel comic superhero to you? Iron Man, Thor, The Hulk, and *The Increaser!*

Good. *It should.* Saint Joseph is one of Earth's mightiest heroes *ever.* He protected Jesus and Mary from King Herod – an evil villain if there ever was one.

Saint Joseph was also the foster-father of Jesus, the greatest and mightiest person there ever was or ever will be ...

The King of Kings ...

The Lord of the Universe.

And St. Joseph helped Jesus become all this.

St. Joseph was *The Increaser!*

The Bible describes Jesus growing up with St. Joseph and Jesus "increased in wisdom and in stature, and in favor with God and man" (Luke 2:52).

Saint Joseph is *all over* the superhero stories, comics, and movies. Do you remember that Superman had a foster-father?

Superman's "heavenly" parents set him adrift in space to save him when their home planet, Krypton, exploded. This is just like what happened to baby Moses. Baby Superman had a space-manger! The manger crash-landed on earth and was found by Jonathan and Martha Kent, who named Superman "Clark Kent." They became Superman's foster parents. Superman "increased in wisdom and in stature" in the home of the Kents.

In *Man of Steel*, a recent Superman movie, Jonathan Kent teaches Superman his greatest lesson: self-sacrifice. Jonathan Kent sacrifices his own life to protect the secret identity of his foster-son.[1]

Most all superhero stories mirror the lives of St. Joseph and Jesus in some way. They can't help it. Jesus' life changed the world. We cannot imagine a hero that is not based on Jesus in some way.

And this all came to be in the humble home of Mary and "The Increaser," St. Joseph.

Saint Joseph, "The Increaser"

ENTRUST YOURSELF TO THE INCREASER: God entrusted His Son to St. Joseph. In these coming days, let us learn why we, too, should entrust ourselves to St. Joseph.

The first reason: If you entrust yourself to St. Joseph, he will "increase" in you all that is good. Saint Joseph will increase your virtues, your holiness, and God's presence in your life.

Saint Joseph is your spiritual father. Saint Joseph is your foster-father, too!

You are a child of St. Joseph. You need to resemble him, especially by imitating his virtues and faithfulness to Jesus and Mary. St. Joseph plays a vital (life-giving) role in your spiritual growth and well-being. *This is the heart of Consecration to St. Joseph.*

Discussion Questions:
1. Do you have a favorite superhero? Who is it?
2. Your favorite superhero — why do you like them so much? Is it their strength, their speed, their intelligence?
3. Can you think of any ways that St. Joseph is better than even your favorite superhero?

Daily Prayers to Recite: Pray the "Our Father" and the Litany of St. Joseph (found on page 15).

DAY 2

Apparitions of St. Joseph

"Don't be afraid!"

Jesus speaks these words to us many times in the Gospels. These words are repeated in the Bible 365 times, one for each day of the year. Jesus probably first heard these words from His father, St. Joseph.

Jesus appeared to the disciples after His Resurrection. Mary has appeared many times in history, especially to children. She appeared to the children in Fatima, to St. Bernadette at Lourdes, to the children at La Salette, and to many, many others. These are all apparitions.

Saint Joseph has also appeared to many people. He appeared at Fatima, as well as Jesus and Mary, on the day of the Miracle of the Sun. This was the day in 1917 when thousands and thousands and thousands of people watched the sun "dance" across the sky. The witnesses had been standing in the pouring rain for hours prior to the Miracle of the Sun. Afterwards, their clothes were suddenly and miraculously dry.

On another rainy day, St. Joseph appeared in Knock, Ireland in 1879, along with Mary, St. John the Evangelist, and a lamb standing on an altar. A large group of people were huddled together in a rainstorm outside their church. Suddenly, Joseph and Mary appeared from Heaven and started glowing brightly. The apparition of St. Joseph was bowing reverently towards Mary and the lamb on the altar.

Though it was raining heavily in Knock that day, the downpour did not touch the figures. Miraculously, the grass beneath them also remained dry.

But the people were not afraid. They called others to see the miracle, and a crowd of many witnesses gathered. People in the town and far away also reported seeing the glow of the figures shining through the darkness and the rain.

Our Lady of Knock

Think about these apparitions.

The apparitions at Our Lady of Knock encouraged people to consecrate themselves to Mary. This created a deep bond of love to Jesus through Mary. This bond would transform people into "apparitions" of Mary. This does not mean we would actually become apparitions, but reflections of Mary in the world. The world needs more apparitions of Mary.

The world also needs more "apparitions of Joseph." We need to radiate the virtues of Joseph. We need more people who resemble Joseph in his protection of the family and the Church, in his purity and patience, and especially in his love for his Son, Jesus.

THE LITANY OF ST. JOSEPH WILL HELP YOU BECOME AN APPARITION OF ST. JOSEPH. You will be praying the Litany of St. Joseph every day of this Consecration.[1] And, each day of the Consecration will now be a line from the litany.

You recite all the virtues of St. Joseph in his litany. This will help you focus on these virtues and begin to reflect these virtues, as an apparition of St. Joseph.

> Let us love Jesus above all, let us love Mary as our mother; but then, how could we keep from loving Joseph, who was so intimately united to both Jesus and Mary? And how can we honor him better than by imitating his virtues? Now, what else did he do in all his life but contemplate, study, and adore Jesus, even in the midst of his daily labors? Behold, therefore, our model.[2]

> — St. Madeleine Sophie Barat

Discussion Questions:
1. Have you ever been really afraid of something? What did it feel like inside?
2. How does it make you feel when Jesus says, "Do not be afraid?"
3. Imagine if Mary or St. Joseph visited you when you were afraid, like in Knock, Ireland. How would you feel?
4. That feeling you just imagined — can you try to remember that feeling whenever you are afraid?

Daily Prayers to Recite: Pray the "Our Father" and the Litany of St. Joseph (found on page 15).

DAY 3

God, the Father of Heaven,
Have Mercy on Us

Saint Joseph was the image of Jesus' heavenly father, God. Do you have a painting or image of a saint in your home? Or, do you have a photograph of someone in your family that has died and is hopefully in Heaven? Do you look at the photograph and remember that person?

In the novel, *The Secret Garden*, Mary Lennox and Colin Craven are the main characters. Mary and Colin's mothers were sisters, both of whom died and are missed very much. Colin keeps a photograph of his mother hidden behind a rose-colored curtain.

Colin tells Mary to draw back the rose-colored curtain to reveal a picture of a beautiful woman who is beautiful and laughing. She also has gray eyes exactly like Colin's own. Colin tells Mary that this is a portrait of his mother. Colin keeps it covered for two contradictory reasons. First, Colin does not like that his mother is laughing while Colin is so ill and unhappy. Second, Colin thinks of his mother as his treasure, and Colin does not want to share his treasure with anyone.

Colin and Mary eventually discover together that Colin's mother still lives on. Colin's mother lives on in her painted image, but especially in her living image, her son. Colin's mother lives on in her son, Colin, in his laughter and his grey eyes, and in their *Secret Garden*.

The picture of Colin's mom brings to life someone in Heaven. God does this for His Son, Jesus, too … and for us.

God gave His Son, Jesus, far more than a painting or a photograph. God gave Jesus a person, a great man, a saint to be His Image on earth. God gave St. Joseph to Jesus. And so, God gives St. Joseph to us all.

Mary Lennox finds Colin Craven sick in bed in *The Secret Garden*

CONSECRATION TO ST. JOSEPH WILL INCREASE THE PRESENCE OF GOD THE FATHER IN YOUR LIFE. When the Heavenly Father sent His Son into the world to save us and make us His children, He selected one person on earth to be the true image of His Fatherhood to Jesus as He was growing up: St. Joseph. Jesus delighted in being called the "son of Joseph" (John 6:42). *So should we!* With Jesus we can contemplate the virtues of Joseph, and increase in our knowledge and appreciation of God the Father in our lives.

> God chose to make Joseph his most tangible image on earth, the depository of all the rights of his divine paternity, the husband of that noble Virgin who is Mistress of angels and men.[1]

> — Blessed William Joseph Chaminade

Discussion Questions:

1. Have you ever been called the "spittin' image" of your mom or dad? Did you know "spittin' image" has nothing to do with spitting? It means "spirit and image." How are you the "spirit and image" of your parents?

2. How is St. Joseph the "spirit and image" of Jesus' father in Heaven?

Daily Prayers to Recite: Pray the "Our Father" and the Litany of St. Joseph (found on page 15).

DAY 4

God, the Son, Redeemer of the World, *Have Mercy on Us*

The idols of false gods cracked and crumbled when Jesus was born into the world, and St. Joseph was there to see it. This happened first when St. Joseph led the Holy Family into Egypt to escape King Herod.

> How thou [St. Joseph] did rejoice to have always near you God himself, and to see the idols of the Egyptians fall prostrate to the ground before him.
>
> — Blessed Januarius Maria Sarnelli

The false gods of Egypt fell down before a baby — the baby Jesus. Jesus was the New Moses. By the power of God, Moses, too, killed all the gods of the Egyptians. The Egyptians worshipped the Nile River as a god. Moses turned the Nile to blood, killing it. The Egyptians worshipped the sun as the god Ra. Moses turned the sun to darkness with an eclipse and put their god to death. Moses killed a different Egyptian god with each of the "Plagues of Egypt."

There are other kinds of idols, too. Saint Joseph can help you destroy these, too.

In Roald Dahl's *Charlie and the Chocolate Factory*, all the kids are horrible, except one: Charlie Bucket. Did you ever notice that each of the other children in *Willy Wonka and the Chocolate Factory* represents one of the Seven Deadly Sins? These sins are their idols.

Terrible things begin to happen to each of these children, because they are so overcome with their misplaced love for things. Do you remember what happens to each of the kids?

Willy Wonka leading the children into the chocolate room,
a "world of [his] imagination."

— Augustus Gloop wants to eat everything, even an entire
  chocolate river. He represents **Gluttony**.
— Veruca Salt wants to own everything. She wants it all,
  from her own Oompa-Loompa to her own golden
  goose. She represents **Greed**.
— Violet Beauregarde wants to be better than everyone.
  She represents **Pride**.
— Mike Teevee ("TV") only wants to watch TV. He represents **Sloth**.
— Willy Wonka, himself, punishes everyone harshly for
  their flaws. Wonka represents **Wrath**.

Do you feel a pang of guilt in your heart when any of
these sins are mentioned? St. Joseph will help you destroy
these sins, these idols, these vices.

How does St. Joseph destroy your vices? He will teach you the virtues. Virtues destroy vices. Saint Joseph will teach you virtues, just as he taught his son, Jesus.

Discussion Questions:
1. What do you think of the kids from Willy Wonka? Do any of their bad habits seem weird to you?
2. Do any of their habits seem familiar to you? Do you have a bad habit like one of the kids from Willy Wonka?
3. How can St. Joseph help you turn your bad habits into good habits? How can St. Joseph help you defeat your vices? And increase your virtues?

Daily Prayers to Recite: Pray the "Our Father" and the Litany of St. Joseph (found on page 15).

DAY 5

God, The Holy Spirit,
Have Mercy on Us

One of St. Joseph's greatest gifts was docility to the Holy Spirit. Docility to the Holy Spirit means that St. Joseph listened obediently to the Holy Spirit. This also means that St. Joseph's obedience was sweet and gentle, like a sheep or a loyal dog. St. Joseph's obedience was not at all forced.

Aslan the lion from *The Chronicles of Narnia* by C.S. Lewis is one of the greatest symbols for Jesus in literature. The second-to-last book of *The Chronicles of Narnia* is *The Silver Chair*.

In *The Silver Chair*, two children, Jill Pole and Eustace Scrubb, stumble into the magical world of Narnia just in time to escape a band of bullies. Almost immediately, Jill meets Aslan. Aslan gives Jill several instructions. Jill hesitates to follow Aslan's instructions, and the problems start.

If Jill had just followed Aslan's instructions, she and Eustace would have quickly accomplished their mission. But Jill was not docile to Aslan's instructions. She was a little confused and a little stubborn. Her disobedience created a big mess that turned into a great adventure. In the end, Aslan used Jill's mistake to make great things happen.

Like Aslan, God gave St. Joseph instructions in St. Joseph's dreams. Unlike Jill Pole, St. Joseph was not stubborn or confused by God's instructions. St. Joseph was docile to God's instructions.

King Herod wanted to kill baby Jesus. King Herod's men killed many, many children. Herod would have killed Jesus, too, if not for St. Joseph's obedience.

Even though the journey seemed dangerous, St. Joseph immediately led his family into Egypt.

Aslan and Jill Pole in *The Silver Chair*

Discussion Questions:

1. Is it sometimes hard to follow instructions? When was the last time you had trouble following instructions from a parent or teacher or even God?

2. Do you know why it was hard to follow instructions? What stops you from following instructions? In what ways are you stubborn? In what ways are you docile?

3. Do you ever feel like God wants you to do something? Or not to do something? Was it hard to do or not do that thing? Why?

4. What stops you from following God's instructions? How can St. Joseph help you with this?

Daily Prayers to Recite: Pray the "Our Father" and the Litany of St. Joseph (found on page 15).

DAY 6

Holy Trinity, One God, *Have Mercy on Us*

The Holy Trinity is the Father, the Son, and the Holy Spirit. The Holy Family of Jesus, Mary, and Joseph is also a trinity. The Holy Family is the earthly trinity.

The Holy Family, the earthly trinity, is also the first Christian church. We want to be members of this church, this family. Being part of this family will prepare us for Heaven. In Heaven, we become members of God's own family, the Holy Trinity.

To become members of the Holy Family, we want to become children of Joseph and Mary and brothers and sisters to Christ. In this consecration, we become children of St. Joseph. We do this to become better children of God, the Father. The head of the earthly trinity, Joseph, will lead us to the heavenly Trinity, to Heaven.

Why do we do this? Because God the Father, Himself, entrusted His Son, Jesus, to Joseph, as well.

This is similar to the story of Ebenezer Scrooge. Scrooge was a greedy old man in Charles Dickens' classic Christmas story, *A Christmas Carol*. Scrooge was especially cruel to his employee, Bob Cratchit.

Bob Cratchit is like St. Joseph. Bob Cratchit is doing his best to protect and provide for his family, though he is very poor. He is so poor that his son, Tiny Tim, is sick and dying.

As you might remember, four ghosts visit Scrooge. The "Ghost of Christmas Future" reveals that Scrooge's cruelty will eventually result in the death of Tiny Tim. Scrooge needs to change his ways to stop Tiny Tim from dying. Scrooge's love for the Cratchit family must "increase."

Scrooge's love for the Cratchit family must "increase" to the point of becoming part of the Cratchit family.

Here are some of the last lines of *A Christmas Carol*:

Scrooge was better than his word. He did it all, and infinitely more; and to Tiny Tim, who did NOT die, he was a second father. He became as good a friend, as good a master, and as good a man as the good old city knew, or any other good old city, town, or borough in the good old world ... and it was always said of [Scrooge] that he knew how to keep Christmas well, if any man alive possessed the knowledge. May that be truly said of us, and all of us! And so, as Tiny Tim observed, God bless Us, Every One!

Scrooge and Tiny Tim, illustration from *A Christmas Carol*

Just like Scrooge became part of the Cratchit family, you should become part of the Holy Family. Like Scrooge, our love for the Holy Family of Jesus, Mary, and Joseph must "increase" to the point that we become members of their family.

Saint Joseph will "increase" our love for the Holy Family. Who better to help us with this than St. Joseph, who is the head of the Holy Family? Who had greater love for his family than St. Joseph?

Discussion Questions:
1. Have you ever thought about the Holy Family of Jesus, Mary, and St. Joseph? Did you know that they are your family, too? Do they feel like family to you?
2. Imagine yourself in that humble house in Nazareth. Jesus is still a baby. Maybe He is playing with toys. St. Joseph is working nearby, hammering or sawing. Momma Mary is tending the fire and baking bread. What do you smell? What do you hear?
3. What does it feel like to be part of the Holy Family? To have Jesus as your brother? Mary as your mother? St. Joseph as your father?

Daily Prayers to Recite: Pray the "Our Father" and the Litany of St. Joseph (found on page 15).

DAY 7

Holy Mary, *Pray for Us*

All Christians belong to St. Joseph because Jesus and Mary belonged to him.

— St. Leonard of Port Maurice

This first week of your Consecration St. Joseph is ending. As the first week ends, our focus shifts from the Holy Trinity — Father, Son, and Holy Spirit — to the Blessed Mother.

You belong to Jesus. Jesus wants you to grow in virtue and holiness. How do you grow in virtue and holiness? Imitate Jesus. How should you imitate Jesus? Imitate His total entrustment to Mary and Joseph.

Why does Jesus want you to entrust yourself to Mary and Joseph?

Well, Jesus is the first one to have entrusted Himself to Mary and Joseph! He, more than anyone else, wants you to love Mary and St. Joseph. He wants you to love them and resemble them.

Jesus loves for you to place roses at the feet of His Mother. What son wouldn't love people to respect and revere his mother? What daughter wouldn't love for people to praise the virtues of her father?

A child will honor those who honor his parents. So, too, will Jesus reward you for honoring His parents.

And what husband would not reward those who praise his wife? St. Joseph will empty the treasures of Heaven for those who honor his wife, Mary.

Here are three important steps for your devotion to Mary:

— Saint Joseph will greatly bless those who love and honor Mary.
— Saint Joseph will "increase" your love for the Virgin Mary.

— Consecration to St. Joseph will make you a Knight of the Holy Queen.

Do you want to be a Knight of the Holy Queen? Mary is the Queen of the Kingdom of Heaven. When you fight for Mary, you fight for the King. Saint Joseph is the most valiant of Mary's knights.

A Queen Knighting a Soldier

Saint Joseph will teach you how to be a Knight of the Holy Queen. When you consecrate yourself to St. Joseph, you are earning your knighthood. When you pray the "Hail Mary" today, pray on your knees. This is how a knight prepares for his or her "knighting."

Discussion Questions:

1. Do you want to serve the Blessed Mother like St. Joseph did? How can you love and honor Mary like St. Joseph did?

2. Do you want to be a knight of the Virgin Mary? What would you do as Mary's knight?

Daily Prayers to Recite: Pray the "Hail Mary" and the Litany of St. Joseph (found on page 15).

DAYS 8-15: OVERVIEW

The Life of St. Joseph

Who was St. Joseph? What were the major moments of St. Joseph's life? What do we remember St. Joseph for?

Take a moment to talk as a family about what you know about St. Joseph. You can list them below:

❖ _____

❖ _____

❖ _____

❖ _____

❖ _____

❖ _____

❖ _____

❖ _____

Don't feel bad if you could not think of something for every line. Let's go over what we know about St. Joseph from the Bible.

SAINT JOSEPH IS NAMED FOR JOSEPH, THE OLD TESTAMENT PATRIARCH. Do you remember Joseph from the Old Testament? His father, Jacob, gave him the coat of many colors, the so-called "amazing technicolor dreamcoat." Joseph's brothers were jealous of him, so they sold him into slavery. Can you imagine ever doing something like that to your brother or sister? Joseph lives as a slave in Egypt and eventually impresses the Pharaoh, himself.

Pharaoh put Joseph in charge of all the granaries of Egypt. Granaries are the places where wheat is stored after it is harvested and the grains of wheat are threshed from the wheat stalks. Granaries are where wheat waits to become bread.

Even though it was mostly a desert, Egypt was the breadbasket of the world during Joseph's time. Egypt produced massive amounts of grain along the Nile River. The world depended on Egypt for this food.

The first Joseph was told in a dream that a great famine was coming. A famine is a time when food is hard to find. The famine did come, but the first Joseph had listened to God. Joseph stored up massive amounts of grain in the years before the famine.

When the famine broke out, Pharaoh told all of Egypt and the rest of the world, "Go to Joseph (*Ite ad Ioseph!*) and do whatever he tells you!" (Gen 41:55). Because Joseph listened to God, he was able to provide bread to the world in a time of great hunger.

The famine even reached Joseph's brothers who had sold him into slavery in Egypt. Joseph's brothers came to Egypt begging for wheat. Joseph's brothers didn't recognize him. They addressed him as "Lord" and were greatly humbled. But Joseph was a great man and did not take revenge on his brothers. Instead, Joseph offered them forgiveness and filled their sacks with grain so his family would not go hungry.

Do you see how the *first* Joseph is like St. Joseph?

The first Joseph gave bread to the whole world, but St. Joseph did something even greater.

The first Joseph protected the world's grain. St. Joseph protected the "Bread from Heaven" — Jesus!

The first Joseph fed the world with bread. St. Joseph protected Jesus, whose flesh was bread "for the life of the world."[1] The whole world ate from bread protected by the first Joseph, but they still died. St. Joseph protected "the living bread which came down from heaven; if any one eats of this bread, he will live forever."[2]

SAINT JOSEPH WAS MARRIED TO THE VIRGIN MARY. The Virgin Mary became pregnant through the Holy Spirit, not St. Joseph. Saint Joseph understood that God had acted in an extraordinary way. Saint Joseph knew his wife, Mary, was very, very close to God. Saint Joseph knew that God dwelled within Mary, making her like the Holy of Holies, the inner-most room of the Temple. One of Mary's own family, the holy priest Zechariah, had been struck dumb while serving in the Holy of Holies. Unworthy men had even died when they drew so near to the presence of God.

Saint Joseph was afraid. He was a humble man. He did not think he was worthy to serve God as Mary's husband. He was not even a priest, like Zechariah. Though descended from kings, he was just a poor carpenter and craftsman.

God sent an angel to St. Joseph to reassure him. The angel spoke to St. Joseph in a dream. The angel told St. Joseph that he should not be afraid to take Mary into his home. Does this remind you of what we say in Holy Mass? "Lord, I am not worthy that you should enter under my roof!"

God sent an angel to tell St. Joseph that, like Mary, he had been chosen for this very special, very great, and very dangerous role in Jesus' life.

SAINT JOSEPH IS A DESCENDANT OF THE PATRIARCHS. Saint Joseph is the last and greatest son of the Patriarchs, except for Jesus, Himself. Saint Joseph's ancestors include King David, Abraham and Isaac, Noah, and Adam and Eve.

SAINT JOSEPH BRINGS MARY TO BETHLEHEM. This is St. Joseph's first major journey with the Holy Family. King David, St. Joseph's ancestor, brought the Ark of God to Bethlehem hundreds of years before. It is now time for St. Joseph to carry the New Ark of God to Bethlehem. There is no room at the inn for the Holy Family, so Mary gives birth in a stable of animals, likely a cave. The Star of Bethlehem stands like a tower of light above the Holy Family, announcing the birth to the world, the shepherds, and the Three Kings.

SAINT JOSEPH FLEES TO EGYPT TO PROTECT THE HOLY FAMILY FROM KING HEROD. The Holy Family is hunted by King Herod. King Herod's soldiers slaughter all the male children of Bethlehem under two years old. Why? King Herod is trying to kill the baby boy that was born in Bethlehem and prophesied to be the King of Kings.

Saint Joseph must lead the Holy Family on a second dangerous journey from Bethlehem, across the wilderness of Sinai, and into a land filled with idols and false gods, Egypt. There are robbers and scoundrels along the way. Saint Joseph protects the Holy Family from all these dangers.

SAINT JOSEPH IS THE FOSTER-FATHER OF JESUS. Jesus grows up in Nazareth as the son of St. Joseph. God gives St. Joseph legal rights to God's Son, such as the right to name Jesus.

Most importantly, Jesus learns how to be a man from St. Joseph. Saint Joseph teaches Jesus all the virtues, responsibilities, and manners of manhood.

DAY 8

Saint Joseph, *Pray for Us*

Saint Joseph is like Adam. Just as Adam was the head of the first family, St. Joseph is head of the Holy Family, the family of the new covenant.

Do you know the Fourth Commandment? "Honor your father and your mother."

Jesus honored all the commandments. He definitely honored the Fourth Commandment. Jesus honored His father and mother, Joseph and Mary. Imitate Jesus in honoring Mary and Joseph.

Saint Joseph's fatherhood is extremely important to our spiritual development. Why? Because we are to imitate Jesus, and Jesus, in His human nature, increased in wisdom and knowledge through the fatherhood of St. Joseph. We need St. Joseph's fatherhood to clothe us in the "proper attire" needed for the wedding feast in Heaven.[1] Heaven is the wedding feast of Jesus and His Bride, the Church.

Have you ever been to a wedding? You probably wore a suit or a special dress, right? The "proper attire" was required.

In the classic tale *Cinderella*, Jesus is like the Prince who pursues his lost love, Cinderella. Cinderella is us, the Church.

In the story, so much depends on Cinderella wearing the "proper attire" for the Prince's ball. Cinderella cannot even attend the Prince's ball until she has the proper ball gown. Cinderella endures the cruelty of her stepmother and stepsisters who deprive her of the proper attire.

It is only with the help of a heavenly visitor, Cinderella's fairy godmother, that Cinderella gets her ball gown and her glass slippers.

At the stroke of midnight, Cinderella runs from the Prince rather than lose her ball gown, her proper attire. Cinderella would be ashamed for the Prince to see her without her proper attire, in her shabby servant's dress.

Cinderella's Fairy Godmother, depicted like an angel

But the Prince pursues his lost love. The Prince searches everywhere for Cinderella.

Ultimately, the Prince only recognizes Cinderella by her "proper attire." The Prince searches the kingdom trying to find the maiden whose feet fit the glass slipper.

The glass slipper, the "proper attire," is like virtue and holiness. Cinderella's stepsisters have no virtue, only vice. It's not just that the stepsisters' feet don't fit into the glass slippers; the stepsisters have no virtue. It is wrong for the stepsisters to clothe themselves in virtue when they are so full of vice.

On the other hand, Cinderella's foot fits perfectly into the glass slipper. This is because Cinderella is so virtuous. She is meek and humble of heart. Cinderella is also kind, gentle, and self-sacrificing.

The "proper attire" is virtue and holiness. You will need to be dressed in this "proper attire" to attend the ball, the wedding feast, in Heaven. Like the Prince, Jesus will find you when you let Him clothe you in virtue and holiness.

Like Cinderella's heavenly helper, her fairy godmother, St. Joseph will help prepare you for the wedding feast. To enter Heaven, you need to resemble your spiritual father, St. Joseph, in his steadfast love for Jesus and Jesus' mother. Saint Joseph will help you dress yourself in the proper attire — virtues and holiness — needed to enter the wedding feast of Heaven.

Discussion Questions:
1. How do you dress for Holy Mass? Why is it important to dress your best for Holy Mass?
2. What is the "proper attire" for Heaven? How are you supposed to dress for Heaven?
3. How can you dress yourself in this "proper attire"? Are these clothes like normal clothes? Can you buy these clothes, like you buy normal clothes? What makes these clothes different?

Daily Prayers to Recite: Pray the "Hail Mary" and the Litany of St. Joseph (found on page 15).

DAY 9

Noble Offspring of David, *Pray for Us*

[God] saw to it that Joseph be born of the royal family;
He wanted him to be noble even with earthly nobility.
The blood of David, of Solomon, and of all the kings of
Judah flows in his veins.

— St. Peter Julian Eymard

Jesus is a king. Jesus is the *King* of Kings. So His father, St. Joseph, must also be a king, right?

But how can that be? Saint Joseph was just a poor carpenter from the poor town of Nazareth – how could he be a king?

Saint Joseph is descended from kings. Joseph's great-great-great-many greats-grandfathers were King Solomon and King David. Not only that, Joseph was descended from the Patriarchs, including Abraham, Noah, and Adam, himself. It is fitting that Joseph's son, the King of Kings, be born from this line of kings and patriarchs.

The prophets foretold that Jesus would be born of King David's line, that Jesus would be a New David. Both Jesus and Joseph are counted as the "noble offspring of David."

This is like in C. S. Lewis' *The Lion, the Witch, and the Wardrobe*. Narnia was once ruled by the evil White Witch. There was an ancient prophecy about the coming of kings and queens that would conquer the White Witch:

When Adam's flesh and Adam's bone
Sits at Cair Paravel in throne,
The evil time will be over and done.

Mrs. Beaver describes the prophecy again, saying "… when two Sons of Adam and two Daughters of Eve sit in those four thrones, then it will be the end not only of the White Witch's reign but of her life."

In Narnia, the White Witch is like the devil. Aslan the Lion conquers her and ends her reign, just like Jesus ends the reign of the devil. The end of the devil and the White Witch's power both happen with the return of the king.

"When Adam's flesh and Adam's bone, sits at Cair Paravel in throne"

And not just any kings! In Narnia and the real world, too, the kings were sons of Adam.

The same thing happens in J.R.R. Tolkien's *The Lord of the Rings*. The books and movies end with *The Return of the King*. Who is the king? There was a prophecy in *Lord of the Rings*, too. The king would be "Isildur's heir." Isildur is the King David of *Lord of the Rings*.

Isildur is the king who picked up his father's, the king's, sword, and defeated the giant Sauron. King David also defeated a giant in battle: Goliath.[1]

So, who was Isildur's heir? Aragorn, son of Arathorn, like Jesus, son of Joseph. Aragorn and his father were the great-great-great-many greats-grandsons of Isildur.

Saint Joseph was the king of the Holy Family. Saint Joseph should be your king, as well, and his Son, the King of Kings.

Discussion Questions:

1. Remember, you, too, are part of the Holy Family. How does it feel being part of the royal family? And not just any royal family, but the most royal of royal families?

2. Do you know that you are a daughter of Eve or a son of Adam? What does this mean to you?

3. How does it feel to be part of the world's first and oldest family? Do you realize that God knew about you from the very beginning? That you, too, are part of the greatest story ever told?

Daily Prayers to Recite: Pray the "Prayer of Blessed Bartolo Longo" (found on page 17) and the Litany of St. Joseph (found on page 15).

DAY 10
Light of Patriarchs, *Pray for Us*

Patriarch means "father." Saint Joseph is the last in a long line of patriarchs from Adam to Noah, Abraham to Jacob, and King David to the New David. The light of God shines through all of these patriarchs and all Christian fathers and culminates in St. Joseph. Saint Joseph is the greatest of the patriarchs — the greatest of all fathers!

> Picture to yourself the sanctity of all the patriarchs of old, that long line of successive generations which is the mysterious ladder of Jacob, culminating in the person of the Son of God. See how great was the faith of Abraham, the obedience of Isaac, the courage of David, the wisdom of Solomon. After you have formed the highest opinion of these saints, remember that Joseph is at the top of the ladder, at the head of the saints, the kings, the prophets, the patriarchs, that he is more faithful than Abraham, more obedient than Isaac, more generous than David, wiser than Solomon, in a word, as superior in grace as he is close to the source, Jesus sleeping in his arms.[1]
>
> — Blessed William Joseph Chaminade

The Patriarchs each bore the light of God to the world until the birth of Jesus, the "light of the world" (cf. John 1). The Patriarchs were torch-bearers. An unbroken line of fathers kept and renewed God's covenant.

They were like the Olympic torch-bearers. The Summer and Winter Olympics bring the world together every four years for contests of sports. The Olympic games begin with the lighting of the Olympic torch. Since the Olympics began in Greece in ancient times, the torch is lit in Olympia, Greece. Torch-bearers then run across the whole world carrying the Olympic torch to the site of the games.

That's a long way to run! When the Olympics were hosted in Beijing, China, the torch-bearers needed to run thousands of miles. How could one person run so far?

Olympic torch bearer

The torch is not carried by just one person, but many. It's a relay. Each torch-bearer runs with the Olympic torch for several miles and then hands it off to the next runner. This continues for days and days until the torch-bearers reach the city where the Olympics are taking place.

God required great fathers, the Patriarchs, to carry His Light through thousands of years and across the world.

The last torch-bearer was St. Joseph. Saint Joseph carried the Blessed Mother across Israel to Bethlehem and then on to Egypt. The Star of Bethlehem rose above them like the world's biggest torch, announcing the arrival of the "light of the world," Jesus.

> If you wish to be close to Christ, we again today repeat,
> "Go to Joseph!" (*Ite ad Ioseph!*)

— Pope Venerable Pius XII

Discussion Questions:
1. How was St. Joseph a torch-bearer? What light did St. Joseph help bear to the world?
2. How can you help bear this light to the world?
3. Do you need to run thousands of miles to be a torch-bearer, or can you start right here, right now?

Daily Prayers to Recite: Pray the "Prayer of Blessed Bartolo Longo" (found on page 17) and the Litany of St. Joseph (found on page 15).

DAY 11

Spouse of the Mother of God, *Pray for Us*

There has never been a man more in love with a woman than St. Joseph was in love with Mary. Mary felt secure and protected with St. Joseph. Saint Joseph was her dragon slayer, her perfect gentleman, and God's own choice of father for her son. Saint Joseph was Mary's knight and warrior. Every wife wants a husband like St. Joseph.

Holy Mother Church also deserves spiritual fathers like St. Joseph. The Church needs priests and bishops that will lead her to truth with boldness and gentleness and away from danger with courage.

The Church is the bride of Christ. She deserves leaders who will lay down their lives for her, chase away the wolves, and slay the dragons. The Church needs men and women who will teach the truth with passion. The Church needs heroes like St. Joseph. *You* are called to be a hero for the Church.

There are many tales of heroic battles, huge armies, and great leaders throughout history, but there is something special about the Medieval period. The Medieval period was full of castles and princesses and knights in shining armor fighting against evil.

In the film *Sleeping Beauty*,[1] Princess Aurora is cursed by the evil witch Maleficent to prick her finger on the needle of a spinning wheel. The princess is protected and hidden from the evil Maleficent by three fairies, who are like her guardian angels or even St. Joseph. Maleficent sends out her minions to find and kill the baby princess just like King Herod hunted baby Jesus. Even when the princess has reached the age of sixteen, Maleficent's minions are still searching for a baby.

Prince Philip hears a beautiful lady singing in the woods. It is Princess Aurora, disguised as a peasant, singing "Once Upon a Dream." Philip falls instantly in love with Aurora's grace and beauty. Aurora, too, falls in love. Neither realize that they have been betrothed in marriage since birth. But "the course of true love never did run smooth."[2]

Maleficent imprisons Aurora in a dark tower where Aurora pricks her finger on the fated spinning wheel. Aurora falls into a deep sleep, only to be awakened by true love's kiss.

The three fairies arm Prince Philip with the tools of a knight: The Sword of Truth and Shield of Virtue. Maleficent surrounds the dark tower with a black "crown of thorns." Maleficent transforms herself into an enormous black dragon.

The dragon, Maleficent, attacks Prince Philip. Philip shields himself from the dragon's fire with the Shield of Virtue. Philip throws the Sword of Truth. His aim is blessed by the fairies, and the sword pierces the dragon's heart, killing Maleficent. Prince Philip then rescues Aurora, awakening her with true love's kiss.

SAINT JOSEPH FIGHTS THE DRAGON, UNLIKE ADAM. Why did Prince Philip succeed? Because Philip sacrificed himself for his true love, like Jesus and St. Joseph. Like Jesus and Joseph, Philip did not run away from the "crown of thorns." Like Jesus and Joseph, Philip was also armed with truth and virtue.

Like Prince Philip, Adam was charged to protect Eve, his true love, and his kingdom, the Garden of Eden, from dragons like Maleficent and Satan. Though he was equipped by God to slay dragons, Adam failed. Saint Joseph, succeeds where his ancestor Adam failed.

Why does the Medieval period with its knights and princesses so capture our imagination? There have been plenty of wars and soldiers in history — why are knights so fascinating? Why are fairy tales, like *Sleeping Beauty*, full of knights?

It is because knights dedicated themselves to God and the Virgin Mary. Soldiers of other times might fight for money, country, or power. Knights fought for God and the Blessed Mother. Knights vowed to fight for Our Lady and Jesus. Knights went on holy quests for Jesus and Mary.

The shield of virtue defends against the fire-breathing dragon

SAINT JOSEPH WAS THE FIRST CHRISTIAN KNIGHT. Who was the first Christian to dedicate himself to protecting the Virgin Mary and Jesus? Who was the very first man to make a vow — marriage vows — to Mary? Who was the first man to undertake a quest for Jesus and Mary? Saint Joseph.

Knights lived by a code of honor called chivalry. The word "chivalry" comes from a French word for knight, *chevalier*. Chivalry provided rules to help men choose the right way of being a warrior. Chivalry helped knights act in accord with Christian teaching even in the heat of battle and the fog of war.

Saint Joseph will teach you to be chivalrous. Saint Joseph will teach you how to dedicate yourself to his true loves, Mary and Jesus, and how to fight for them.

Discussion Questions:

1. What dragons are attacking you, your family, and the world?

2. How can you fight these dragons? What sword will you use to slay the dragons? What sword did St. Joseph use?

3. What is chivalry? How will St. Joseph teach you to be chivalrous?

Daily Prayers to Recite: Pray the "Hail Mary" (found on page 17) and the Litany of St. Joseph (found on page 15).

DAY 12

Chaste Guardian of the Virgin, *Pray for Us*

It was necessary that divine Providence should commit [Mary] to the charge and guardianship of a man absolutely pure.[1]

— St. Francis de Sales

Saint Joseph teaches us about a very important virtue: Chastity. To be chaste is to have self-control, control over your passions, emotions, and body. Chastity preserves the purity of the human heart. God calls all of us to chastity. Without the self-control of chastity, our passions will control and enslave us. Without chastity, we act like wild animals.

SAINT JOSEPH IS PURE OF HEART. To be chaste means you are pure of heart. Jesus tells us, "Blessed are the pure of heart, for they will see God."[2] Saint Joseph gazed on the face of God for years and years. Saint Joseph and Mary were the very first people to gaze on the face of baby Jesus. Not only that, no one since Moses — none of the prophets or kings — had beheld God's face.

Saint Joseph now looked upon the face of God daily. So many times, St. Joseph beheld the most beautiful of sights: baby Jesus sleeping in his arms or asleep in Mary's arms. Saint Joseph must have had the most chaste and pure eyes of any father or husband who ever lived.

Unfortunately, today's world is full of sights and sounds that attack our chastity and purity. Perhaps now more than ever, we need St. Joseph to guard our eyes against impure images and vulgar music.

Illustration of *Snow White*'s Evil Queen from *Europa's Fairy Book* (1916)

Our world — or more specifically, Satan — is like the Evil Queen in *Snow White*. We are born spotless and white as pure snow like "Snow White." Snow White is also like the Virgin Mary. Snow White is like a mother, caring for the "seven dwarves." Snow White teaches the seven dwarves about virtue, because each of the seven dwarves represent one of the Seven Deadly Sins. Snow White is beautiful because she is virtuous and pure of heart.

The Evil Queen asks her mirror, "Mirror, mirror, on the wall, who's the fairest of them all?" Though the Evil Queen desires to be "the fairest of them all," the mirror reveals that it is Snow White, instead. The Evil Queen is a slave to her passions, and desires that Snow White be killed. The Evil Queen even asks the Huntsman to bring her the heart of Snow White.

Saint Joseph is like the Huntsman, who rejects the Evil Queen and protects Snow White's heart. Saint Joseph will protect your heart, as well.

SAINT JOSEPH IS A GENTLEMAN AND CHIVALROUS. Yesterday, you read about chivalry. Chivalry was the code of honor that protected the purity of knights in battle. Chivalry also taught knights to protect the purity of others, especially women.

As you read yesterday, St. Joseph is the first Christian knight. Saint Joseph is also the first Christian gentleman. Saint Joseph is our perfect model of a chivalrous gentleman. He was married to the most pure and beautiful woman in the world, Mary. Saint Joseph protected her purity and reverenced her beauty.

Saint Joseph will teach you to be a protector of purity and defender of beauty, instead of users and abusers of those whom you are charged to protect and guard.

Family Activity: Can you guess which deadly sin is connected to each dwarf?

You can use the acronym PLAGGES, like "plagues," to help you remember the Seven Deadly Sins: **P**ride, **L**ust, **A**nger (or wrath), **G**reed, **G**luttony, **E**nvy, and **S**loth.

Now that you can remember the Seven Deadly Sins, connect each of the seven dwarves with the deadly sin they represent. Some may be more obvious than others.

Here are the names of the seven dwarves by Disney reckoning: Sleepy, Grumpy, Doc, Happy, Bashful, Sneezy, and Dopey.

Don't look at the answers on page 146 until you are ready![3]

Daily Prayers to Recite: Recite together, if possible, the excerpt from Psalm 51 below and pray the Litany of St. Joseph (found on page 15).

> Create in me a clean heart, O God,
>   and put a new and right spirit within me.
> Cast me not away from thy presence,
>   and take not thy Holy Spirit from me.
> Restore to me the joy of thy salvation,
>   and uphold me with a willing spirit.

DAY 13

Foster Father of the Son of God,
Pray for Us

Saint Joseph is the "foster father" of Jesus, at least that is how we describe their father-son relationship in English. The Latin term is *Filii Dei Nutricie*. This literally means "Nurturer of the Son of God." Wow, that sounds much warmer and heartfelt than "foster father."

Saint Joseph was given this important role of "Nurturer of the Son of God" by God through an angel. An angel of the Lord appeared to St. Joseph in a dream, saying,

> Joseph, son of David, do not fear to take Mary as your wife, for that which is conceived in her is of the Holy Spirit; she will bear a son, and you shall call his name Jesus, for he will save his people from their sins.

These words from the angel are packed with meaning. One important detail is that God is giving St. Joseph the authority to name Jesus. By the Jewish law, this makes St. Joseph the adopted father of Jesus.

In the classic novel, *Anne of Green Gables*, a red-headed orphan girl named Anne is adopted by an aging brother and sister named Matthew and Marilla Cuthbert. Anne instantly fell in love with the Cuthbert's home, Green Gables, and the lovely island they lived on, Prince Edward Island. But there was a big problem.

Marilla did not want to adopt Anne and take her into their home. The Cuthberts had asked the orphanage to send them a boy, not a girl. A boy would be able to help Matthew with all his farm chores. Matthew really needed help with the farm, because he was already an old man. Even so, it was Matthew's tender-heartedness that saved Anne from being sent back to the orphanage.

Matthew opened his heart to Anne almost instantly and loved her as if Anne were his own child. Like St. Joseph,

Matthew was a man of very few words. Marilla argued convincingly that Anne was no good to them since she could not help Matthew with the farm. Matthew responded "We might be of some good to her." Eventually, Marilla was moved by Matthew's compassion.

Anne of Green Gables illustration: Matthew presents Anne to Marilla

Matthew was right to take a risk on the orphan, and his trust in God was greatly rewarded. Anne went on to live a beautiful life on Prince Edward Island. Anne was also at Matthew's side when he died. Likewise, St. Joseph is the patron saint of a happy death, because Jesus and Mary were at his side when he died.

God was calling Matthew to a special role in an orphan's life: foster father. Like St. Joseph, Matthew did not at first understand, but his trust in God was richly rewarded.

SAINT JOSEPH WILL ADOPT YOU AS YOUR SPIRITUAL FATHER. The love between father and child does not end at death. This love endures forever. Jesus continues to be the Son of Joseph in Heaven. The Church still describes Jesus as "Son of Joseph." Jesus will always be the "Son of Joseph." You, too, can be a "son of Joseph" or "daughter of Joseph." Ask St. Joseph to adopt you, just like he adopted Jesus.

As St. Joseph took care of Jesus while on earth, St. Joseph will take care of you during your life. Ask St. Joseph to be your protector, provider, and educator, as he protected, provided for, and educated Jesus.

Discussion Questions:
1. Will you ask St. Joseph to adopt you? Is there anything stopping you from asking St. Joseph to adopt you?
2. How do you ask St. Joseph to adopt you? Do you think this consecration is a way to ask St. Joseph for his help and fatherhood?

Daily Prayers to Recite: Pray the "O Joseph, Virgin Father of Jesus" prayer Pope St. Pius X (found on page 18) and the Litany of St. Joseph (found on page 15).

DAY 14

Zealous Defender of Christ, *Pray for Us*

[St. Joseph] protects those who revere him and accompanies them on their journey through this life – just as he protected and accompanied Jesus when he was growing up.[1]

— St. Josemaría Escrivá

God tasked St. Joseph with defending Jesus from many dangers, threats, and snares of the devil. And with God's help, St. Joseph succeeded in keeping his wife and son safe. St. Joseph wants to watch over you, too. St. Joseph wants to help you arrive safely home, both your earthly home and your ultimate home in Heaven.

Saint Joseph always defended Jesus and Mary. He was a dutiful watchman and kept guard over the Holy Family. Jesus said, "I am the Good Shepherd. The Good Shepherd lays down his life for the sheep."[2] Jesus first learned about the Good Shepherd from his father. Saint Joseph shepherded Mary and Jesus to safety and away from the wolves sent by King Herod. Again, and again, St. Joseph laid down his life for Jesus and Mary.

In the movie *Finding Nemo*, Marlin and his son Nemo are clownfish who live on the Great Barrier Reef. Marlin is really protective of his son, because Marlin's wife and all his other children were killed in a barracuda attack. Marlin's protectiveness embarrasses Nemo in front of his whole class. Nemo then accepts a dare to swim beyond the reef and touch the bottom of a boat with his fin. Away from the safety of the reef, a scuba diver captures Nemo in a net and takes him away.

This begins the father's great adventure to rescue his son. Marlin also leaves the safety of the reef to rescue and find Nemo. Marlin swims to the seafloor asking different schools of fish for help and befriending a blue tang fish named Dory.

Dory says she knows where Nemo's boat went, but Marlin quickly realizes that Dory has no short-term memory. Things then go from really bad to worse.

Father and Son: Marlin and Nemo

Sharks! Marlin and Dory run into a great white shark named Bruce, plus a hammerhead and a mako shark.

After a series of explosions, Marlin and Dory then find themselves hanging over the edge of a deep ravine. After escaping an anglerfish, they barely escape a school of stinging jellyfish.

Marlin and Dory awaken to find they have been saved by a sea turtle named Crush who help them ride the East Australian Current. The fast-moving current will take Marlin and Dory to Sydney, where they will hopefully find Nemo.

Facing obstacle after obstacle, Marlin is relentlessly brave as he searches for his lost son, Nemo. Marlin is a "zealous defender" of Nemo. Marlin lays down his life again and again for Nemo, like St. Joseph. Marlin never gives up trying to protect and find his lost son. St. Joseph, too, would never give up protecting Jesus and searching for Him.

SAINT JOSEPH WILL NEVER GIVE UP PROTECTING AND DEFEND-
ING YOU. You have nothing to fear with St. Joseph at your side.
What is there to be afraid of with such a zealous defender as
your father who loves you? St. Joseph held the Maker of the
Universe in his hands. St. Joseph fed the Creator of the heav-
ens. In his role as earthly father to Jesus, St. Joseph lovingly
commanded the Son of God. Heaven and earth obeyed him.
All hell trembles before him!

> Joseph's name will be a name of protection all during
> our lives.[3]

> — Blessed William Joseph Chaminade

Discussion Questions:
1. How is *Finding Nemo* the story of a father?
2. Nemo's father, Marlin, had to face challenge after challenge to find Nemo. He risked his life again and again
   for Nemo. How did St. Joseph do this for Jesus?
3. How can St. Joseph do for you what he did for Jesus?
4. How can you defend Christ like St. Joseph did?

Daily Prayers to Recite: Pray the "O Joseph, Virgin Father
of Jesus" prayer by Pope St. Pius X (found on page 18) and
the Litany of St. Joseph (found on page 15).

DAY 15

Head of the Holy Family,
Pray for Us

Jesus and Mary not only bent their wills to Joseph's, for he was head of the Holy Family, but they lovingly surrendered their hearts to him as well.[1]

— St. Peter Julian Eymard

Saint Joseph was head of the Holy Family. This means he is the leader of the Holy Family. Does this seem strange? Mary was the greatest human that ever lived. Jesus was God, Himself. Why would St. Joseph be the head of the Holy Family? This is because God established the family, and God ordered the family with fathers as the head of the family.

SAINT JOSEPH IS THE PERFECT FATHER. Saint Joseph's fatherly example teaches us the meaning of a father's strength, authority, and headship. Saint Joseph teaches us that being the head of the family is not about being boss. It's about service to others — service unto death. It's about the father laying down his life for his family.

Saint Joseph was the leader and head of the Holy Family. Saint Joseph teaches us that leadership flows from self-sacrifice. Saint Joseph also teaches us that families can be fragile and need protection. The life of the entire world depended on the lives of the Holy Family, so the whole world depended on St. Joseph's headship.

This is like the movie *The Lion King*. The lives of all the animals were connected and depended on the leadership of the "lion king." Mufasa, the good king of the lions, taught his son, Simba, many things. Mufasa taught his son about how all life is connected in the "Circle of Life." Mufasa taught Simba about his future kingdom:

Look, Simba, everything the light touches is our kingdom. ... A king's time as ruler rises and falls like the sun. One day, Simba, the sun will set on my time here, and will rise with you as the new king.

Simba is amazed and asks his father, "What about that shadowy place way out there?" Mufasa answers, "That's beyond our borders. You must never go there, Simba." The king is teaching Simba, the future king, that even the king must abide by the law.

Lion King Mufasa and Simba overlooking their kingdom

Mufasa's last lesson to Simba was self-sacrifice. Simba was tempted to go to the "shadowy place" and to violate the law. To save Simba's life, Mufasa is forced to sacrifice his own.

Tragically, Mufasa would have survived but for the treachery of the king's evil brother Scar. After Mufasa's death, Simba runs away. In the absence of the true kings, the evil Scar rules the kingdom.

Darkness comes to the kingdom. The rich and fruitful kingdom is laid to waste by the bad king. Hunger and evil reigns. Scar is the opposite of Mufasa, because he sacrifices others instead of himself, even to the point of murder.

To save the kingdom, Simba must learn to be king — the head of the family — through self-sacrifice.

Like Mufasa, St. Joseph taught Jesus about self-sacrifice. Jesus was born into a world of darkness, ruled by Satan and evil kings, like King Herod or Scar.

HUSBANDS AND FATHERS NEED TO IMITATE ST. JOSEPH. At the Last Supper, Jesus gave the Eucharist to His Apostles and the whole world. Jesus told them He was laying down His life for them, and then He washed their feet.

Who do you think taught Jesus about this? Jesus' feet would have been first washed by St. Joseph. When Mary rested after giving birth, St. Joseph would have bathed baby Jesus. During their long journey into Egypt, St. Joseph would have lovingly washed the sandy, dirty feet of Mary and Jesus.

MAKE ST. JOSEPH THE SPIRITUAL HEAD OF YOUR FAMILY. What would be a good daily reminder that St. Joseph is the spiritual head of your family? Get a statute or beautiful image of St. Joseph for your home. Place it in a prominent location to remind everybody to ask St. Joseph for help. Learn to ask him for help all the time, and you will see what a difference St. Joseph's help makes.

> Dear Brothers and Sisters, the sacrament which unites you to each other, unites you in Christ! It unites you with Christ! "This mystery is a profound one!"[2] [Jesus] comes to you and is present in your midst and dwells in your souls. In your families! In your homes! Saint Joseph was well aware of this. For this reason, [St. Joseph] did not hesitate to entrust himself and his family to God. By virtue of this trust, [St. Joseph] completely fulfilled his mission, entrusted to him by God for the sake of Mary and his son. Supported by the example and protection of St. Joseph, offer a constant witness of devotion and generosity.[3]
>
> — Pope St. John Paul II

Discussion Questions:

1. In *The Lion King*, father teaches son. What did Mufasa teach Simba? How did Mufasa teach Simba? How did Simba learn his father's lessons?

2. How did Jesus teach the Apostles about self-sacrifice? How was the Eucharist a part of this?

3. How did St. Joseph serve his family? How did St. Joseph wash their feet?

4. How can you remind your family to ask St. Joseph for help?

Daily Prayers to Recite: Pray the "O Joseph, Virgin Father of Jesus" prayer Pope St. Pius X (found on page 18) and the Litany of St. Joseph (found on page 15).

St. Joseph statue for the home

DAYS 16-22: OVERVIEW
St. Joseph, Father of Virtues

Picture yourself in the workshop of St. Joseph, the Carpenter, and the home of the Virgin Mary. Sit down on the cool floor, as Jesus did, and learn from these greatest of all saints.

SAINT JOSEPH WILL INCREASE YOUR VIRTUES. Do you know what virtues are? We will be learning about the virtues from St. Joseph. We will be learning how St. Joseph will "increase" the virtues in us.

There are Seven Heavenly Virtues, a group of three and a group of four. There are three Theological Virtues: faith, hope, and charity. There are also four Cardinal Virtues: justice, courage (also called fortitude), temperance, and prudence.

In the coming days, we will be going over each of these and how St. Joseph will "increase" these virtues in you.

SAINT JOSEPH WILL DEFEAT YOUR VICES. Do you know what vices are? In this section, we will be learning from St. Joseph how to defeat the vices.

There are also seven vices. These are often called the Seven Deadly Sins: pride, lust, anger, greed, gluttony, envy, sloth.

Is that a lot to remember? Remember the trick we learned on Day 12? Use the made-up word PLAGGES – like "plagues" because these sins are plagues – to remember the Seven Deadly Sins. Try it again. P – pride, L – lust, A – anger, G – greed, G – gluttony, E – envy, S – sloth.

VIRTUES AND VICES COME IN PAIRS. When St. Joseph increases one of your virtues, he is also defeating one of your vices. There are Seven Contrary Virtues that pair with the Seven Deadly Sins and defeat them. These seven are a little different from the last seven. It's a little confusing, so let's make a game out of it.

Do you think you can figure out which virtue defeats which vice?

Here is a list of the vices, a list of blanks, and a Word Bank of the Seven Contrary Virtues that defeat the Seven Deadly Sins. We have described some of these virtues, but not all. Fill in the blank with the virtue that defeats the vice in the Word Bank. The answers are on page 146:[1]

Seven Contrary Virtues:
Charity
Humility
Patience
Courage (or Fortitude)
Chastity
Temperance
Generosity

❖ Pride   _____

❖ Lust   _____

❖ Anger   _____

❖ Greed   _____

❖ Gluttony_____

❖ Envy   _____

❖ Sloth   _____

In the days ahead, we will be covering most all of these virtues, plus some extras.

DAY 16

Joseph Most Just, *Pray for Us*

> [St. Joseph] won for himself the title of "The Just Man," and thus serves as a living model of that Christian justice which should reign in social life.[1]
>
> — Pope Pius XI

What does it mean to call St. Joseph a "just" man? The classical definition for the virtue of justice is "giving to another their due."[2] Justice to God is especially important. We owe God everything. Giving God His "due" means giving everything to God. This can be said of St. Joseph because he dedicated his whole life to his family, which included God.

Saint Josemaría Escrivá explained why Scripture praises St. Joseph as "a just man":

> Saint Joseph was an ordinary sort of man on whom God relied to do great things. He did exactly what the Lord wanted him to do, in each and every event that went to make up his life. That is why Scripture praises Joseph as "a just man." In Hebrew a just man means a good and faithful servant of God, someone who fulfills the divine will,[3] or who is honorable and charitable toward his neighbor.[4] So a just man is someone who loves God and proves his love by keeping God's commandments and directing his whole life towards the service of his brothers, his fellow men.[5]

What about you? Can you be described as "just"? Do you give to God his due? Do you give to others their due?

This is like the story of *The Little Red Hen*. Once upon a time, there was a little red hen, who lived on a farm. The little red hen was friends with a lazy dog, a sleepy cat, and a noisy yellow duck. The little red hen found some wheat seeds. She decided to plant them and harvest the wheat.

Little Red Hen baking bread

Each step of the way, the little red hen asked for help. Each time, her friends responded the same way:

"Not I," barked the lazy dog.

"Not I," purred the sleepy cat.

"Not I," quacked the noisy yellow duck.

The little red hen asked, "Who will help me take the wheat to the mill to be ground into flour?" And then, "Who will help me bake the bread?" Each time, the little red hen's friends responded the same way:

"Not I," barked the lazy dog.

"Not I," purred the sleepy cat.

"Not I," quacked the noisy yellow duck.

And finally, when the bread was finished, the tired little red hen asked her friends, "Who will help me eat the bread?"

"I will," barked the lazy dog.

"I will," purred the sleepy cat.

"I will," quacked the noisy yellow duck.

"No!" said the little red hen. "I will." And the little red hen ate the bread all by herself.

The little red hen was just, even if she was not charitable. She gave to each what was their due. The lazy dog, sleepy cat, and yellow duck were each due nothing.

Saint Joseph and Mary raised the boy who would one day become bread for the world. Like the little red hen, St. Joseph and Mary were often alone in raising Jesus. Worse than alone, the Holy Family was persecuted by King Herod and the devil, himself.

Saint Joseph perfectly guided the Holy Family through these persecutions. How did he do it?

> To be just is to be perfectly united to the Divine Will, and to be always conformed to it in all sorts of events, whether prosperous or adverse. That St. Joseph was this, no one can doubt.[6]

> — St. Francis de Sales

SAINT JOSEPH WAS PERFECTLY UNITED TO GOD'S WILL. People struggle to understand God's will for their lives. Knowing God's will is like having a map of your life, a map that tells you exactly where to go and where not to go.

If you had perfect understanding of God's will, you could walk onto a battlefield like a Jedi Master from *Star Wars*. You could dodge blaster fire and bullets before they were even fired.

Saint Joseph understood God's will in a very special way. Saint Joseph always acted in accord with God's will. Because of this, St. Joseph listened to God and brought Mary into his home, when other men would have run away. Because of this, St. Joseph evaded all of King Herod's men.

SAINT JOSEPH WILL INCREASE IN YOU THE VIRTUE OF JUSTICE. Ask St. Joseph to teach you to be "a just man" or "a just woman." Ask St. Joseph to help you understand God's will for your life. He will help you steer clear of all dangers. Saint Joseph will also help you keep your eyes focused on Mary and the face of Jesus, as he did. With these two as your north star, you will never wander off God's path for you.

Discussion Questions:

1. What is the virtue of justice?
2. Can you be too just?
3. As in the story of the *Little Red Hen*, sometimes justice is knowing when to say yes and to say no. Who should you always say "yes" to? When would you need to tell somebody "no"?
4. How can you know God's will for your life week-by-week, day-by-day, moment-by-moment?

Daily Prayers to Recite: Pray the "Children's Memorare to St. Joseph" prayer (found on page 18) and the Litany of St. Joseph (found on page 15).

DAY 17

Joseph Most Chaste, *Pray for Us*

Jesus said, "Where your treasure is, there will your heart be also."[1] Saint Joseph has three treasures: Jesus, Mary, and you. These three treasures consume St. Joseph's heart more than anything else. The heart of St. Joseph is the heart of a loving father. Saint Joseph's heart is a home for you. You have the key to his heart. You can seek shelter in St. Joseph's most chaste heart.

SAINT JOSEPH WILL HELP GUARD YOUR HEART FOR CHASTITY. Lust is the main enemy of the hearts of men. Lust is a deadly sin. Lust attacks hearts more now than possibly ever before. Lust-filled acts greatly offend God, ruin families, and cry out to heaven for justice.

St. Dominic Savio

Saint Dominic Savio died when he was a boy, but that did not stop him from being a saint. Even though he was just a boy, he did many saintly and heroic things in his short life. Many of these happened at school. Several times St. Dominic stood up to his friends who wanted to do bad things.

Saint John Bosco ran a school for boys. One of these boys was St. Dominic. Saint John Bosco wrote down many stories about St. Dominic. A boy was visiting Bosco's school, and he had brought with him a "magazine with bad pictures." A group of fascinated boys were looking at the bad magazine. Saint Dominic snatched the magazine and tore it up, saying, "You know well enough that one look is enough to stain your souls, and yet you go feasting your eyes on this." Saint Dominic also told them, "I know it is fascinating, but your soul will feast one day on a much more satisfying feast."

Like St. Dominic, St. Joseph wants to guard your heart from bad experiences, sights and sounds that will rob you of your purity.

SAINT JOSEPH WILL HELP GUARD YOUR EYES FOR PURITY. There are many girl saints that fought for purity, as well. There's St. Maria Goretti, St. Lucy, St. Agnes, and St. Philomena – all of these suffered torture and martyrdom to preserve their chastity. Saint Gemma Galgani stands out for the way she guarded her eyes. It's a hard claim to make — especially when St. Lucy's eyes were actually taken from her by the Romans — but it's true.

We can learn so much from St. Gemma, but perhaps the most important thing is the desire to love God with all our hearts. She wrote, "O, love, O, infinite love! O love of my Jesus! Let Your love penetrate my all. From You I want nothing else."[2]

From childhood, she was the master of her eyes. She vowed to keep her eyes lowered to avoid temptation.

Once, she let her eyes wander to the dress of the girl sitting next to her at Mass. She was curious about the stitching and needlework. Her guardian angel scolded her for this.

St. Gemma Galgani

Saint Gemma was also harassed by the devil. As she was finishing her dinner one evening, the devil appeared to her in an impure form and threatened her. Gemma turned pale and ran out the back door to a deep tank of water in the garden. It was winter, and the water was icy cold.

Making the Sign of the Cross, Gemma threw herself into the freezing water. She would have died or been seriously injured, but a hand drew her shivering from the water.[3]

SAINT JOSEPH WILL INCREASE IN YOU THE VIRTUE OF CHASTITY. Saint Joseph will help you guard your eyes and heart like St. Gemma and St. Dominic, despite all the world's temptations. Saint Joseph kept the Holy Family safe and pure despite all the evils fighting against him. As a child of St. Joseph, he will protect you, as well.

Discussion Questions:
1. Why did St. Dominic Savio fight so hard to guard the other boys' eyes from the "magazine with bad pictures"?
2. Why did St. Gemma jump into the icy water? And why did she make the Sign of the Cross?
3. How can St. Joseph, St. Dominic Savio, and St. Gemma Galgani help you guard your eyes and heart?

Daily Prayers to Recite: Pray the "Children's Memorare to St. Joseph" prayer (found on page 18) and the Litany of St. Joseph (found on page 15).

DAY 18

Joseph Most Prudent, *Pray for Us*

What is prudence? Prudence isn't just another virtue. Prudence is the "charioteer of the virtues," the *auriga virtutum* in Latin.[1] Of course, you might be asking, "What's a charioteer"? The charioteer drives the chariot, which is pulled by a team of horses. Before cars, chariots were the fastest way to drive people around.

Look at the chariot race below:

Jean Léon Gérôme. "Chariot Race." 1876

Those horses look pretty wild, right? All these horses are supposed to be running in the same direction, but that's not what happens sometimes. A lot depends on the one driving the horses: the charioteer.

The other classical virtues — temperance, justice, and fortitude — are like the horses that pull the chariot. The horses are so strong they could rip the chariot into pieces. They could even rip the charioteer into pieces, if he is not careful.

Driving a chariot is dangerous business. Vices are very dangerous, too. Your vices hurt you and your loved ones. That's why we need strong virtues.

Did you know that the first Christian martyr of Ireland was a charioteer? Saint Odran was the charioteer for none other than St. Patrick.

Odran heard a rumor that people were trying to kill St. Patrick. A wicked pagan chieftain fiercely hated St. Patrick and was plotting to kill him. The chieftain hated Patrick, because Patrick had destroyed Crom. Crom was a pagan idol worshipped by the people of Ireland.[2]

Odran learned that the wicked pagans were planning to kill Patrick while he rode as a passenger in his chariot.

Ancient Irish Chariots of Clonmacnoise (9th century)

Out of prudence, Odran did not tell Patrick what he knew. Odran knew that St. Patrick would willingly give up his life for him. Instead, Odran asked Patrick to take the reins of the chariot. Odran told Patrick that he needed a short rest. Not long after switching places with Patrick, Odran was mistaken for Patrick and struck by a spear.

Due to Odran's self-sacrifice, the spear that was intended for Patrick killed Odran instead. Saint Patrick survived and lived to spread the Gospel across all Ireland, converting all the pagans.

Like St. Patrick needed Odran, you need prudence. Prudence can be your faithful charioteer like St. Odran.

As the charioteer of the virtues, prudence guides the other virtues. The charioteer cracks a whip if the horses are going too slow. The charioteer also pulls back on the horses with the reins if the horses are going too fast. Prudence, the charioteer, tells the horses how fast to go.

Prudence stops the other virtues — temperance, justice, and fortitude — from going too fast. We just learned about being just and what is justice. Too much justice, however, can be bad. Justice needs to be slowed down by mercy and compassion. This is the job of prudence, the charioteer.

SAINT JOSEPH WILL INCREASE IN YOU THE VIRTUE OF PRU-DENCE. So far, we have been talking about natural prudence. Saint Joseph, the superhero, will teach you *super*-natural prudence.

A man of just human prudence would not take the place of his friend and bishop, like St. Odran did, and step into the path of a spear.

A man of just human prudence would not arise from a dream and flee with his family to Egypt, like St. Joseph did. Saint Joseph is no ordinary man. The Holy Spirit gave St. Joseph superpowers, including supernatural prudence.

Supernatural prudence does not try to avoid suffering. Instead, supernatural prudence heroically embraces suffering and the Cross of Jesus. Saint Joseph will help you become a superhero like him.

Discussion Questions:
1. How is the virtue of prudence like a charioteer?
2. How did St. Patrick's charioteer, St. Odran, practice prudence and self-sacrifice to save St. Patrick's life?
3. What are the other virtues? How could St. Odran have used these to save St. Patrick? And why was prudence the best way?

Daily Prayers to Recite: Pray the "Children's Memorare to St. Joseph" prayer (found on page 18) and the Litany of St. Joseph (found on page 15).

DAY 19

Joseph Most Courageous, *Pray for Us*

Saint Joseph desired nothing but the things of Heaven. He did not fear his own death. Saint Joseph would gratefully lay down his own life for those of Jesus and Mary. This is why St. Joseph is called "Most Courageous."

"Joseph Most Courageous" is also translated as "Joseph Most Valiant" or "Joseph Most Strong."

SAINT JOSEPH WILL INCREASE YOUR COURAGE. Saint Joseph took his family on a long journey to Bethlehem and then an even longer journey to Egypt. He knew that they might be attacked by robbers along the way, and he was prepared to fight for his family. In Egypt, St. Joseph needed to defend his family from pagan rituals, idol worshippers, and sorcerers. Saint Joseph was not intimidated.

Church history is full of brave men and women. Do you know about St. Joan of Arc? Though a young girl, she led the armies of France into battle. She was very courageous.

Do you know the wonderful story about St. George and the dragon? In a place called Silene in Libya, a venom-spewing dragon lived in the murky depths of a pond.[1] It spewed its venom over the farms and poisoned the lands. The people offered the dragon tribute to stop its attacks.

At first, the dragon took just two sheep every day. Then, the dragon started taking a man and a sheep. Finally, the dragon began taking their children. All the children's names were put in a bowl and chosen, one by one, to be sacrificed to the dragon. Eventually, the king's daughter was chosen. The king offered all his gold and silver to spare his daughter, but the people refused. The daughter was sent to the dragon's lake, dressed as a bride, to be fed to the dragon.

Saint George arrived as the dragon was emerging from the dark pool. She told him to run, but he vowed to protect the girl. Saint George charged the dragon on horseback and wounded it with his spear.

Saint George told the king's daughter, "Fear not, my child, and throw your girdle about the dragon's neck!" She did as St. George said, and the dragon became obedient and followed her like a little dog on a leash.

St. George and the dragon

Saint George and the king's daughter returned to town with the dragon on a leash. Saint George told the town, "If you all become Christians, I will kill the dragon for you." The king and about fifteen thousand men were baptized that day. Saint George beheaded the dragon with his sword, and the king built a church dedicated to the Blessed Mother on the spot. A spring of healing water flowed from the church's altar and blessed the town for all its days.

Like St. George, St. Joseph tells us to "fear not." And like St. George, St. Joseph will help us bring to Jesus those who do not know him. Like the spring of healing water that flowed from the church's altar, the life-giving spring of baptism will well up inside those who come to know Jesus.

SAINT JOSEPH WILL INCREASE IN YOU THE VIRTUE OF FORTI-TUDE. What are you afraid of? Your spiritual father, St. Joseph, was a poor man and unknown by the world. Yet the demons and sorcerers of Egypt were terrified of the courageous heart of St. Joseph.

Jesus learned courage by watching St. Joseph. Saint Joseph gave Jesus an example of manly love, courage, strength, and fortitude. Saint Joseph will do the same for you. With St. Joseph as your spiritual father, you have nothing to fear.

Before His suffering and death, Jesus told His disciples, "In the world you will have trouble, but take courage, I have conquered the world."[2] Set your face to Heaven and never look back.

Discussion Questions:
1. What did the town give the dragon originally to try and satisfy it? Why does the dragon always want more and more? Why is the dragon never satisfied? What does this tell us about sin?
2. How did St. George slay the dragon? What did the town need to do before St. George could kill the dragon?
3. What is the virtue of fortitude?
4. What did St. Joseph do that took a lot of courage?
5. How can St. Joseph increase our courage and take away our fear?

Daily Prayers to Recite: Pray the "Children's Memorare to St. Joseph" prayer (found on page 18) and the Litany of St. Joseph (found on page 15).

DAY 20

Joseph Most Obedient, *Pray for Us*

If you want to know St. Joseph's obedience, look at how
he rose at night at the angel's voice and, giving no care
to hunger, hardships, or cold, went to Egypt where he
led a hard life until the next command of God.[1]

— St. Joseph Sebastian Pelczar

Obedience is a very important virtue. People misunder-
stand obedience, though. Obedience is not the opposite
of freedom. Obedience is not slavery. Obedience is a needed
part of life. Try to imagine the world without obedience or
rules or laws. What would roads be like without stop signs and
traffic lights? What would music sound like?

Obedience to God is extremely important. God doesn't
need our obedience; we need it. God will answer our prayers,
if we just listen to him. The Bible is filled with examples
of people who followed God's law and instructions obediently *and* without understanding why. Think about Father
Abraham.

God promised Abraham that his family would be massive. But Abraham was over one hundred years old when his
wife had their first child, Isaac. And then, God asked Abraham to sacrifice Isaac!

With amazing obedience, Abraham obeyed God's command. Abraham's obedience was rewarded when God spared
his son. And through Isaac, Abraham became the father to all
of Israel — thousands and thousands and thousands of people.

Adam and Eve are examples of disobedience. The disobedience of our first parents plunged the whole world into
sin. God asked Adam and Eve to obey the law: do not eat
the forbidden fruit. The devil attacked Adam and Eve's faith
in God. Satan asked, "Did God really say you would die?"[2]
Faith is essential for obedience. This is why Adam and Eve
fell from grace.

Abraham is asked to sacrifice his child Isaac

SAINT JOSEPH IS A MODEL OF OBEDIENCE. Our new parents, St. Joseph and Mary, succeed where Adam and Eve failed. Joseph and Mary trusted in God and were willing to suffer and even die to obey God. Their love and trust in God was simple and beautiful:

> Why was St. Matthew so keen to note Joseph's trust in the words received from the messenger of God, if not to invite us to imitate this same loving trust?[3]

— Pope Benedict XVI

SAINT JOSEPH WILL INCREASE IN YOU THE VIRTUE OF OBEDIENCE. Remember, St. Joseph is the "Increaser." So many people today are repeating the words of the devil, "Did God really say [fill in blank]?" Did God really say you shall not kill, even unborn babies? Did God really say that marriage was just for a man and a woman? Did God really say honor your father and mother? Did God really say to love Him above all things, even money or video games or yourself? God truly did command all these things.

As simple as it may seem to obey all these rules, we need help with the virtue of obedience. Saint Joseph will help us. Saint Joseph will increase our trust, love, and obedience.

Discussion Questions:
 1. Why is Abraham an example of obedience? Why was Abraham going to kill his son, Isaac? Isn't this a very bad thing?
 2. How was St. Joseph "most obedient"? How did St. Joseph obey God?

Daily Prayers to Recite: Pray the "Children's Memorare to St. Joseph" prayer (found on page 18) and the Litany of St. Joseph (found on page 15).

DAY 21

Joseph Most Faithful, *Pray for Us*

Saint Joseph is a model of Faith. What is Faith? Faith is one of three Theological Virtues: faith, hope, and charity. The Bible tells us that faith is "evidence of things not seen."[1] Despite many trials and hardships, St. Joseph was always faithful to Mary and Jesus.

Dr. Seuss wrote a great story about faith being tested. Have you ever read *Horton Hears a Who?*

One day, Horton the Elephant is splashing in a pool in the Jungle of Nool. Suddenly, Horton hears a small voice coming from a speck of dust. Horton cannot see who is talking to him, but he believes it's some tiny person calling for help.

Horton feels very protective of the fragile tiny life flying around on the speck of dust, because, "after all, a person's a person, no matter how small."

Horton places the speck on a very soft clover and vows to protect it. Horton's kangaroo friends think he is crazy to believe in the tiny life. News spreads quickly through the Jungle of Nool that Horton is a fool.

Horton soon hears another voice coming from the speck. It's the Mayor of Whoville. There's a whole tiny town on the tiny speck! Horton again vows to protect the tiny town that nobody can see.

Monkeys snatch the clover from Horton and run away through the treetops. Monkeys pass the clover to a black-bottomed eagle named Vlad.

Horton chases after the eagle as it flies and flies into the night with Whoville hanging from its beak.

Horton begs the eagle, "Please don't harm all my little folks, who have as much right to live as us bigger folks do!"

The next morning, the eagle dropped the Whoville clover into a field of clovers a hundred miles wide. Horton searched, hour after hour, until he found his friends on the three millionth flower.

Horton searching through the field of clover

The animals of Nool are very upset with Horton for protecting the tiny lives. They gang up on Horton, promise to tie him up, and boil the dust speck in "a hot steaming kettle of Beezle-Nut oil."

Horton begs Whoville to make some noise to prove they exist. The Mayor of Whoville calls a big meeting. They cry out in fear: "We are here! We are here!"

But the animals of Nool don't hear it. They gang up to attack and tie-up Horton. Horton calls out again to Whoville to make more noise. The Whos blow on bazookas, "on clarinets, oom-pahs and boom-pahs and flutes."

But only Horton can hear it. Horton asks if every Who is doing their best. The Mayor ran from house to house to make sure every Who was making all the noise they could. The Mayor found one little boy who was not making a sound. The Mayor carries the boy to the top of the Eiffelberg Tower, and tells him:

"We've GOT to make noises in greater amounts! So, open your mouth, lad! For every voice counts!"

The little Who boy shouted "YOPP!" That one, small extra Yopp did it. Whoville is heard. The animals finally believe Horton.

Horton cries out in joy, "They've proved they ARE persons, no matter how small. And their whole world was saved by the Smallest of All!" The whole Jungle of Nool vows to protect the small lives "no matter how small-ish."

Do you see how Horton is a model of faith like St. Joseph? Remember, faith is "evidence of things not seen." Horton believes in things he cannot see and cannot understand. Also like St. Joseph, Horton saves an entire world. Horton does this while everybody is doubting and attacking him. Both St. Joseph's and Horton's faith is tested under extreme pressure.

SAINT JOSEPH WILL INCREASE YOUR FAITH. Today's world is like the Jungle of Nool. It's not easy to be faithful to Jesus. The world does not want you to trust Jesus, hope in His promises, or love Him. If you live according to the teachings of Jesus, you will be ridiculed and mocked — just like Horton, mocked even by some members of your family and some of your friends.

The world especially loves to ridicule you when you say, as Horton did, "a person's a person, no matter how small." That is, when you stand against the killing of unborn babies by abortion. An unborn baby is a person, too, even though they are very small.

Saint Joseph also had to protect his family from people killing babies: The Slaughter of Innocents. Trying to kill Jesus, King Herod instructed his men to kill all the newborn babies.

Imitate the faith and loving trust of St. Joseph. Be steadfast, trusting, bold, and intrepid in your faith:

> It is precisely the intrepid faith of St. Joseph that the Church needs today in order to courageously dedicate herself to the urgent task of the new evangelization. [2]

> — Pope St. John Paul II

Discussion Questions:
1. Why is Horton the elephant an example of faithfulness?
2. What is faith?
3. What does "evidence of things not seen" mean?
4. How was St. Joseph "most faithful"? What did St. Joseph do that was faithful?

Daily Prayers to Recite: Pray the "Children's Memorare to St. Joseph" prayer (found on page 18) and the Litany of St. Joseph (found on page 15).

DAY 22

Mirror of Patience, *Pray for Us*

The flower of Israel [St. Joseph] had the faith of Abraham, the piety of David his ancestor, the wisdom of the prophets, a patience more heroic than that of Job and of Tobias, and a zeal greater than that of Elijah for the glory of God.

— Blessed Gabriele Allegra

Patience is one of the hardest virtues. This is especially true in a world of social media. Everything we want is at our fingertips, but our fingertips are always itching to check for the next notification and update.

And then there's social media. Everything we want is at our fingertips, but our fingertips are always itching to check for the next notification, like, tweet, and Snapchat.

All this convenience is re-wiring our brains. Our anxiety is increasing, and our patience is disappearing. We crave screen time. Without it, we get nervous, twitchy, and anxious.

Blessed are all those who wait on the Lord.

— Isaiah 30:18

Waiting? Patience? When do we learn these things? Go to Joseph to learn patience.

SAINT JOSEPH IS A MODEL OF PATIENCE. Life was not easy for St. Joseph. Saint Joseph had nothing at his fingertips to see if there would be storms on the way to Bethlehem. Saint Joseph couldn't check GPS to find his way to Egypt. There was no internet for him to find a room at the inn. Saint Joseph's mission required a lot of waiting.

Saint Joseph endured so many trials of patience. Natural patience could not have carried St. Joseph so far. Saint Joseph was gifted with supernatural patience, a gift from the Holy Spirit.

Remember St. Dominic Savio? When St. Dominic was eleven, he gave a great example of patience, as he patiently endured a false accusation..

A boy in St. Dominic's class put snow and trash in the classroom stove. This was a mean thing to do. The stove was supposed to warm the classroom during the cold winter months. Instead, smoke filled the classroom. Everybody started choking. The teacher was furious.

When the angry teacher asked who did it, the boy who did it accused St. Dominic. The teacher scolded St. Dominic in front of his class and threatened to expel him.

What do you think St. Dominic did? Saint Dominic was silent while the teacher scolded and humiliated him. He did not tell on the culprit or defend himself.

Later, the teacher found out that St. Dominic was innocent and apologized for scolding him. The teacher asked St. Dominic why he did not defend himself. Saint Dominic said, "I knew that the other boy was in trouble for other things. I remembered how Our Lord had been unjustly accused. I hoped that if I kept silent, he would be given another chance."

Jesus was also accused of crimes he did not commit. He could have summoned legions of angels to save His life. Instead, He allowed Himself to be killed for our crimes, our sins.

SAINT JOSEPH WILL INCREASE YOUR PATIENCE. Saint Joseph was a model of patience for his Son. Saint Joseph, too, was persecuted by King Herod, even though he was innocent. Saint Joseph endured many trials with patience to keep the Holy Family safe.

You, too, will experience many trials in your life. These trials will test your patience. Every day your patience will be tested. Every day is a new opportunity to learn patience. God allows this to help you grow in virtue.

A great way to grow in patience is to be merciful. Be merciful to people even when it's their fault, not yours — like St. Dominic Savio did. When you are asked to endure trials and hard times, imitate the patience of St. Joseph and St. Dominic.

Ask God for the grace to love your neighbor. Be kind, peaceful, and merciful. When your family is testing your patience, be pleasant and merciful. When your friends or classmates irritate you, show mercy. Patience and mercy always leads to victory.

Discussion Questions:
1. What would you have done if you were falsely accused like St. Dominic?
2. What is special about the way St. Dominic responded to the other schoolboys and to his teacher?
3. How can you be more like St. Dominic?
4. What did St. Joseph endure patiently?

Daily Prayers to Recite: Pray the "Children's Memorare to St. Joseph" prayer (found on page 18) and the Litany of St. Joseph (found on page 15).

DAYS 23-33: OVERVIEW

Saint Joseph, Minister of Salvation

As the Church's Liturgy teaches, [St. Joseph] "cooperated in the fullness of time in the great mystery of salvation" and is truly a "minister of salvation."[1]

— Pope St. John Paul II

In the days ahead, you will learn about how St. Joseph is still active in the world. You will also learn how St. Joseph will help you be active in the world for the salvation of souls. This is the great work of St. Joseph and all Christians: to save souls.

This is why St. Joseph is a model for all men, because he is called both "Minister of Salvation" and "Model of Workmen." He shows you that it is important to work both to provide for your families and for the salvation of souls.

Saint Joseph needed to work hard to provide for his family, because the Holy Family was very poor. When St. Joseph brought Mary and Jesus to the temple, he could not afford to buy a lamb. Let that sink in. St. Joseph could not buy a lamb for his son, the Lamb of God.

This is why St. Joseph is also called "Lover of Poverty." It is not that the Holy Family's poverty — or any family's poverty — is good. "Blessed are the poor in spirit," Jesus tells us. Whether you are rich or poor, blessed are you when you love no *thing* more than you love God.

Jesus spent most of his life with St. Joseph and Mary in their little home in Nazareth. Saint Joseph will open the door to this little house to you, so you, too, can experience the simple glory of life in that house. This is why St. Joseph is called the "Glory of Domestic Life."

Maybe most important of all, St. Joseph helps take care of our families as the "Pillar of Families." God entrusted the Holy Family to St. Joseph to keep them safe. We ask St. Joseph for this help, too — to keep our families safe and holy.

We ask St. Joseph to minister to us when we are sick, when we are suffering or afflicted, and even in death. This is why St. Joseph is called the "Hope of the Sick," "Comfort of the Afflicted," and "Patron of the Dying."

Think about St. Joseph's death, too. Who was he surrounded by when he died? Jesus and Mary. This is why St. Joseph is called the "Patron of the Dying" and the patron of a "happy death." When we die, we hope to see all our family and loved ones that we have lost. Above all, though, we hope to see Jesus, Mary, and St. Joseph.

DAY 23

Lover of Poverty, *Pray for Us*

> Truly, I doubt not that the angels, wondering and adoring, came thronging in countless multitudes to that poor workshop to admire the humility of him who guarded that dear and divine child, and labored at his carpenter's trade to support the son and the mother who were committed to his care.[1]
>
> — St. Francis de Sales

The Holy Family was poor. Very poor. Saint Joseph was so lowly and poor that when the Three Wise Men entered the stable in Bethlehem, they did not even acknowledge St. Joseph's presence.[2]

We see how poor St. Joseph was again and again in the Gospels. After Jesus' birth, St. Joseph brought Mary to the Temple in Jerusalem to be purified. Saint Joseph was supposed to buy a lamb for a burnt offering,[3] but he could not afford it. Because they were so poor, the Holy Family was allowed to buy two turtledoves, instead.[4]

Jesus was *the* Lamb of God. The Lamb of God was too poor to buy a lamb for God.

This is why St. Joseph is called "Lover of Poverty." He sacrificed everything for God. Saint Joseph willingly suffered poverty for the love of his Son and wife.

Jesus said, "Blessed are the poor in spirit, for theirs is the kingdom of heaven."[5] Is Jesus saying that poverty is a good thing? No, St. Joseph and Jesus both knew all too well that poverty was very hard. Babies born into poverty often did not live, in Jesus' time and now.

Jesus is saying that we cannot be stuck on things. We need to be detached from earthly things to see the beauty of heavenly things. This is the virtue of poverty. We cannot love things more than God.

Illustration from *Little Women*, "They All Drew Near to the Fire"
by Essie Willcox Smith (1922)

Have you ever read *Little Women* or seen a movie version of it? The women of *Little Women* are the March family, a mother and four daughters who are struggling in poverty while their father is a soldier away at war. There were other families who were even poorer than the March family. Though the March family often went without enough to eat, one sister, Beth, would share their food with another, poorer family, the Hummel family.

Beth was very different from her sister Amy. Amy used the family's rag money to buy popularity at school and avoid the embarrassment of her family's poverty. Amy used the rag money to buy limes, which were a rare treat at that time. The more limes a child had at school, the more popular they were.

Unlike Amy, Beth was beautifully detached from earthly things. On one rare occasion, the March family received a feast for Christmas. Beth convinced her mother and sisters to give away their feast to a poor family. Beth even convinced Amy to donate her part of the Christmas feast.

SAINT JOSEPH WILL INCREASE YOUR DETACHMENT. Saint Joseph will help you to be poor in spirit. Saint Joseph will teach you to love God more than things, like toys and money. He will help you detach from your love of things.

By detaching yourself from things, what are you attaching yourself to? Or Who? Jesus.

When not distracted by material things you can grow closer to Jesus. Jesus will be able to lead you better, when your heart is not divided between Jesus and things. You will be able to trust Jesus more and listen to the Holy Spirit better.

Discussion Questions:
1. What does it mean to be a "Lover of Poverty"? Does that mean that poverty is good?
2. What is your favorite thing? Could you give it away?
3. Are you more like Beth or Amy March? How can you become more like Beth and less like Amy?

Daily Prayers to Recite: Pray the Litany of St. Joseph (found on page 15) and the "Prayer Taught to the Children at Fatima" (found on page 18).

DAY 24

Model of Workmen, *Pray for Us*

At the workbench where [St. Joseph] plied his trade together with Jesus, Joseph brought human work closer to the mystery of the Redemption.[1]

— Pope St. John Paul II

God loves an honest and hard worker. The devil hates him. The devil first attacked the human family in the workplace — that is, the Garden of Eden that God gave Adam and Eve to tend and to keep.

The Garden of Eden was an orchard full of trees, not just the Tree of Knowledge of Good and Evil and the Tree of Life. God told Adam to take care of the garden and to defend it, but Adam failed. Adam let the dragon, Satan, come into the garden. Adam should have slayed the dragon, but he failed.

Because of Adam's failure, God cursed the land. Mankind would have to work much harder to grow food after the Garden of Eden. "By the sweat of your brow," God said, "you will eat bread."[2] God did this so man would learn the fruits and blessings of hard work.

Unlike Adam, St. Joseph did not fail. Saint Joseph does not fail. He is a hard worker, and he taught Jesus to work "by the sweat of his brow." Saint Joseph taught Jesus the beauty and dignity of hard work.

Satan hates hard workers and hard work. Satan especially hates that, out of love, God humbled Himself, became man, and worked hard alongside St. Joseph doing manual labor as a carpenter.

When Jesus told us the following about work and labor, He really knew what He was talking about:

Come to me, all who labor and are burdened, and I will give you rest. Take my yoke upon you, and learn from me, for I am meek and humble of heart, and you will find rest for your souls. For my yoke is easy, and my burden is light.[3]

Saint Joseph will teach you to work hard, and St. Joseph will work hard to help you. This means St. Joseph will help you "increase" in diligence and the other virtues, and sometimes a little something extra ...

SAINT JOSEPH HELPS THE SISTERS OF LORETTO. In 1873, the Sisters of Loretto, a group of nuns, started a girls' school in Santa Fe, New Mexico. Many families wanted to send their girls to their school, so the school grew quickly in size. The sisters needed a new chapel built.

Once the chapel was finished, the sisters looked up to their choir loft and realized they still needed a staircase to get to it. The sisters couldn't climb a ladder because of their long habits or dresses. The sisters couldn't build a normal staircase, because there was no room.

The sisters needed a miracle. They started praying a novena for St. Joseph's help.

On the ninth day of the novena, a mysterious man came to the sister's convent. He said he wanted to build them a staircase. The mysterious man had only one request: he wanted to work alone behind closed doors. The Sisters of Loretto hired the man.

It took three months for the man to build the staircase. As soon as he finished, he disappeared. No one saw him leave town. The sisters couldn't find him. They even placed an advertisement in the newspaper. The sisters went to the lumberyard to pay for the wood the man had used for the staircase.

The mysterious man had never gone to the lumberyard. No wood from the lumberyard had gone to the chapel.

If this was not surprising enough, the sisters began to take a good look at their new staircase. It was very odd.

The sisters remembered that the mysterious man had only used a T-square, saw, hammer, and some other basic tools to build the staircase.

With only these simple tools, the man had built a spiral staircase. The staircase looked like it was just floating in air. The staircase had no center support or columns or nails!

The wood of the staircase was recently studied.[4] Scientists discovered that the spruce wood of the staircase could not be found anywhere in New Mexico. The spruce wasn't found anywhere in all of North America. The spruce was only to be found across the world in the Holy Land. The spruce the mysterious man used would have been the kind St. Joseph would have had in Israel in Nazareth.

The Sisters of Loretto believed that St. Joseph himself had visited them and had built their miraculous staircase.

The Miraculous Staircase, Santa Fe, New Mexico

SAINT JOSEPH WILL TEACH YOU TO WORK HARD. Learning the virtues is hard work. Hard work is hard work. Saint Joseph will work hard to help you. He will help you learn the joy of completing a task even when it becomes difficult or seemingly impossible. This is the virtue of diligence.

Why did Jesus do manual work for most of his years on earth, instead of spiritual work and working miracles?

Jesus did this to teach us that work is honorable and pleasing to God.

Saint Joseph also serves as the model workman for those who work hard for the salvation of souls, especially deacons, priests, bishops, and religious sisters and brothers.

Like manual work, spiritual work can also be very hard. Saint Joseph teaches us, as he taught Jesus, how to work hard with our hands and how to work hard to save souls.

> Let us ask St. Joseph to foster staunch vocations for our Lord.[5]
>
> — St. Peter Julian Eymard

> [St. Joseph] took [the child Jesus'] little hands and raising them to heaven he said: "Stars of heaven, behold the hands which created you; O Sun, behold the arm that drew you out of nothingness."[6]
>
> — Blessed William Joseph Chaminade

Discussion Questions:

1. Why does Satan hate hard work? Why does Satan especially hate that Jesus should grow up with a carpenter as a father?
2. Why is the Loretto staircase so amazing?
3. Miracles happen all the time. Have you ever experienced a miracle? Do you know anybody that has?
4. How can St. Joseph teach you the value of hard work?

Daily Prayers to Recite: Pray the Litany of St. Joseph (found on page 15) and the "Prayer Taught to the Children at Fatima" (found on page 18).

DAY 25

Glory of Domestic Life, *Pray for Us*

Domestic means "home." To be the "Glory of Domestic Life" means to be the "Glory of Home Life." Saint Joseph is the "Glory of Domestic Life," because he was a great father, husband, and head of the family. Saint Joseph was a great blessing to the home in Nazareth, and he will be a great blessing to your home, too.

How does a father affect his children? Think about it. Talk about a few things that you received from your father: looks, habits, virtues, etc. Do you look like your dad? Do you have your dad's eyes or smile?

Do you remember when we talked about the phrase "spittin' image" a couple weeks back? Have you heard of somebody described as the "spittin' image" of their father? This phrase has nothing to do with "spit." "Spittin' image" is short for "spirit and image." All children are the spirit and image of their earthly and heavenly fathers.

This is especially true of Jesus. Jesus bears the "spirit" of God the Father — the Holy Spirit. Jesus is also the "image" of God the Father. Jesus also bears a resemblance to his foster father, St. Joseph.

Saint Josemaría Escrivá once gave a homily about St. Joseph called "In Joseph's Workshop." Escrivá describes the wonderful relationship St. Joseph and Jesus had as father and son. His homily is paraphrased below:

> Saint Joseph passed on his own skill as a craftsman to Jesus. Jesus worked in Joseph's workshop and by Joseph's side. What kind of man Joseph must have been – what grace he must have had – that Joseph could fulfill God's task for him: raising the Son of God!
>
> Jesus must have resembled Joseph. Jesus must have resembled Joseph in his way of working, in the features of his character, in his way of speaking. Jesus' eye for detail, the way Jesus sat at a table and broke bread, the

way Jesus used everyday situations to teach about God – all this is a reflection of the influence of St. Joseph.

This is a great mystery. Jesus is a man who speaks with a particular accent found in a remote part of ancient Israel, who resembles St. Joseph in His way of speaking and acting, and Jesus is also God. But who can teach God anything? Yet, Jesus is still a man who lives a normal life. First, Jesus is a child, then a boy in Joseph's workshop, then finally a man in the prime of his life. As Luke tells us in his Gospel, "Jesus advanced in wisdom and age and grace before God and men."[1]

Growing up, Jesus' master during his daily life was St. Joseph. Joseph was full of affection and always ready to deny himself to take better care of Jesus and Mary. This is what we strive for in our spiritual lives, and St. Joseph did it in that little house in Nazareth every single day. St. Joseph was master of the interior life – being in and with Jesus, being one with Jesus, and talking to Jesus all the time. St. Joseph did this every single day of his life until he died.

This is why St. Joseph is the just man, the holy patri-arch, and the master of the interior life. This is why we should "go to St. Joseph." With St. Joseph, the Christian learns what it means to belong to God and to take his place in the world, sanctifying the world. Get to know St. Joseph and you will find Jesus.[2]

SAINT JOSEPH WILL OPEN TO YOU THE HIDDEN YEARS OF JESUS. Saint Joseph is the saint of the hidden years of Jesus. The hidden years are the thirty years of Jesus' life, between His birth and public ministry, that we don't know much about. Jesus spent these years — almost his entire life — with St. Joseph and Mary in that little house in Nazareth.

Saint Joseph will open the door to his home in Nazareth to you, so you, too, can also spend your days playing with the child Jesus and working with the man Jesus.

This is why St. Joseph is the "Glory of Home Life," because St. Joseph did daily in his home what all saints have ever strived for: interior union with Jesus. St. Joseph will open the door to you, so you can spend your days with the Holy Family, too.

St. Joseph, Custodian of the Two Hearts

Imagine hearing the laughter of the child Jesus, the patter of his bare feet on the floor, the first time Jesus struck a hammer to wood. Imagine sitting in the kitchen of Mary and around the dinner table with the Holy Family. Saint Joseph will bring you into this "glorious" home life.

Discussion Questions:
1. Can you imagine growing up in the workshop of St. Joseph, like Jesus did? What do you think Jesus learned in St. Joseph's workshop?
2. How old are you? Can you imagine Jesus at your age? What would it be like to play with Jesus? Take a moment to imagine this.
3. How can St. Joseph open up Jesus' childhood to you?

Daily Prayers to Recite: Pray the Litany of St. Joseph (found on page 15) and the "Prayer Taught to the Children at Fatima" (found on page 18).

DAY 26

Guardian of Virgins, *Pray for Us*

Saint Joseph lived for thirty years with the two greatest virgins that ever lived: Jesus and Mary. Saint Joseph guarded and protected Jesus and Mary. Virginity is a great treasure. Virginity also needs to be guarded. There are many people and dangers in this world that try to rob us of this great treasure: the purity of our bodies.

Saint Thérèse of Lisieux had a great devotion to St. Joseph. Saint Thérèse especially looked to St. Joseph as a "Guardian of Virgins." Here is what she wrote in her diary:

> I prayed to St. Joseph to watch over me. From my childhood, my devotion to him was mingled with my love for the Blessed Virgin. Each day I recited the prayer, "O Saint Joseph, father and protector of virgins." It seemed to me that I was well protected and completely sheltered from every danger.[1]

> — St. Thérèse of Lisieux

Through prayers to St. Joseph, St. Thérèse was also cured of a childhood illness. You will be learning more about her miraculous cure in a few days.

Do you remember the story of *101 Dalmatians*? What was it about?

101 Dalmatians tells the story of a cruel and evil woman named Cruella de Vil. Cruella's last name is actually the word "devil." That's how bad she was.

101 Dalmatians is also the story of a husband and wife, Roger and Anita. Roger had a boy Dalmatian named Pongo. Anita had a girl Dalmatian named Perdita. Dalmatians are white dogs with lots of black spots, as pictured:

Dalmatian puppies

Roger and Anita fell in love and were married. Their dogs, Pongo and Perdy, also fell in love and had puppies. Lots of puppies. Lots and lots and lots of puppies. In total, 101 Dalmatian puppies.

Remember the villain of *101 Dalmatians*? This is how cruel and evil Cruella de Vil was — she wanted to kill all those cute and innocent puppies. Not only that, Cruella wanted to make fur coats from their skin.

Don't worry! Roger and Anita and Pongo and Perdita save their puppies from Cruella. They protect the innocence of their puppies.

Who are Roger and Anita and Pongo and Perdita like? St. Joseph! They guard and protect the innocence of their children and those entrusted to them.

Cruella's attempt to kill all the innocent puppies was like the Slaughter of the Innocents. Do you remember the Slaughter of the Innocents from the Bible? What was it?

The Slaughter of the Innocents was the killing of all children under the age of two around Bethlehem by King Herod. Herod was trying to kill the baby boy who was prophesied to be king and overthrow King Herod. The baby boy was Jesus. Saint Joseph saved Jesus from this slaughter. Saint Joseph is the guardian of innocents, the guardian of virgins.

SAINT JOSEPH WILL HELP YOU BE A GUARDIAN OF VIRGINITY AND PURITY. Entrust yourself to St. Joseph. He will help guard your eyes, thoughts, heart, and body from impurity.

Stay close to St. Joseph, and you will find less and less pleasure from watching shows and movies that are crude or unclean. Good shows, movies, books, music, and pictures lift up your soul. They are uplifting. Bad shows, movies, books, music, and pictures darken and stain your soul. Entertainment that offends God or degrades women, you will like less and less.

Saint Joseph will help guard you from darkness. You will also know light from darkness.

Everyone is tempted to sin against purity. Some more than others. In St. Joseph, everyone has a guardian and protector. Turn to St. Joseph in times of temptation. He will help you grow in innocence and purity. Ask St. Joseph's help every time you are tempted. He will help keep your heart pure and chaste.

Discussion Questions:

1. Why is Cruella de Vil like the devil? How did she attack the innocence of the puppies? Why does the devil attack our innocence?

2. What was the Slaughter of the Innocents? How did St. Joseph protect Jesus from this slaughter?

3. Why are we tempted to sin against purity? How can St. Joseph guard your purity?

Daily Prayers to Recite: Pray the Litany of St. Joseph (found on page 15) and the "Prayer Taught to the Children at Fatima" (found on page 18).

DAY 27

Pillar of Families, *Pray for Us*

W hat is a pillar? What do pillars do? Pillars are posts or columns that hold up a building or a building's roof. They are like the legs of a table. Pillars provide a foundation and support. A building is only as strong as its foundations.

Pillars along the facade of a building

Jesus tells us a parable about building on strong foundations in Matthew 7:24-27:

> Everyone who hears these words of mine and does them will be like a wise man who built his house upon the rock; and the rain fell, and the floods came, and the winds blew and beat upon that house, but it did not fall, because it had been founded on the rock.

> And everyone who hears these words of mine and does not do them will be like a foolish man who built his house upon the sand; and the rain fell, and the floods came, and the winds blew and beat against that house, and it fell; and great was the fall of it.

A strong family, like a strong home, is built "upon the rock," not the sand. This rock is a stone pillar. The stone pillar of the Holy Family was St. Joseph.

Saint Joseph knows a thing or two about building a house on strong foundations. Saint Joseph is known for being a carpenter, but he was also a builder of houses and other buildings. Saint Joseph knew how to build a house from top to bottom, from roof to pillar.

SAINT JOSEPH WANTS TO BE THE PILLAR OF YOUR FAMILY. For your family to stand on a firm foundation, for your family to be unshakable, your family needs St. Joseph. Saint Joseph will teach your family the importance of prayer, mutual respect, purity, honesty, forgiveness, and love. Most importantly, St. Joseph will teach your family to place God front and center and above all things.

SAINT JOSEPH LOVES THE FAMILY! Saint Joseph, the Pillar of the Family, teaches us why fatherhood, motherhood, and childhood are all so important. Saint Joseph is the saint of the childhood and early hidden years of Jesus. Saint Joseph shows us what a family should be like. That's why St. Joseph is so important, especially today. Because the family is under attack. The family needs a guardian, like St. Joseph.

The Blessed Mother, when she appeared at Fatima, told us that the last attack will be against the family. This is happening right now.

A family is a father, a mother, and a child or children, like the Holy Family. Some people are trying to change the meaning of family. Some people are teaching that a family can have two fathers or two mothers. This is not true. We need St. Joseph to protect families from these false teachings.

We need St. Joseph to teach us how fathers and mothers can become more holy. Families are the pillar of civilization, and St. Joseph is the pillar of families. The world needs more men, more fathers like St. Joseph, and the world will be renewed.

I saw Jesus assisting his parents in every possible way, and also on the street and wherever opportunity offered, cheerfully, eagerly, and obligingly helping everyone. [Jesus] assisted [St. Joseph] in his trade, and devoted himself to prayer and contemplation. [Jesus] was a model for all the children of Nazareth.[1]

— Blessed Anne Catherine Emmerich

Discussion Questions:

1. What is the pillar of our entire civilization and our whole world?
2. How can St. Joseph become the pillar of your family?
3. How are people trying to change the definition of family?

Daily Prayers to Recite: Pray the Litany of St. Joseph (found on page 15) and the "Prayer Taught to the Children at Fatima" (found on page 18).

DAY 28

Comfort of the Afflicted, *Pray for Us*

Do you know the seven Corporal Works of Mercy? The works of mercy help us to see Jesus in people that are hurting or need help, people who are "afflicted" by something, like hunger or thirst.

The works of mercy help us to know, love, and serve Jesus better. They help us be devout followers of Jesus.

Almost daily, St. Joseph performed the works of mercy to Jesus and Mary directly. This is why St. Joseph is called "Comfort of the Afflicted." How blessed was St. Joseph!

Family Activity: It's really important to remember all seven Corporal Works of Mercy. Can you name all seven? Before you read further, try to name as many works of mercy as you can as a family.

How did you do? Let's work on remembering all seven. Here is a "handy" phrase for remembering all seven Corporal Works of Mercy: THIS HaND. Here you go:

Thirsty: Give drink to the Thirsty.
Hungry: Give food to the Hungry.
Imprisoned: Visit the Imprisoned.
Sick: Care for the Sick.

Homeless: Shelter the Homeless.
Naked: Clothe the Naked.
Dead: Bury the Dead.

Does that help? Don't let the 'a' in hand confuse you. It's just there to help spell out "hand." There are also the seven Spiritual Works of Mercy, in case you were wondering.[1]

St. Joseph, the Increaser

SAINT JOSEPH WILL COMFORT YOU IN DIFFICULT TIMES. There will be times in all our lives when we are "afflicted" or in misery. This world is a valley of tears. Everyone is going to suffer. There is no way around it.

No matter what life brings, St. Joseph will be there to comfort you, as he comforted Jesus and Mary. Saint Joseph suffered a lot in his life, but his sufferings were for Jesus and Mary. This made St. Joseph's sufferings sweet and easier to bear.

Saint Joseph is a kind and loving father. Saint Joseph comforts everyone who asks his help in times of affliction. Saint Joseph is a very special father.

> Let us commend ourselves to our good father, St. Joseph, who is the Patriarch of troubled people, since he himself went through so much trouble.[2]

— St. Joseph Marello

A loving father, like St. Joseph, comforts his children when they are suffering. It is important to know you can always go to your dad when you are hurting. Sometimes, when you scrape your knee or something really bad happens, you just need your dad. Even if you have lost your dad or your dad is not around or you have been hurt by your dad, you will always have St. Joseph.

Saint Joseph is your spiritual dad. He loves you. He will never hurt you. Saint Joseph would give his life for you a million times over.

God wants you to rest in St. Joseph's fatherhood. Saint Joseph will never abandon you. No matter what experience you have had with fathers, St. Joseph will be there for you.

Run to your spiritual father in times of trouble. Pour out your heart to him. Tell him your troubles. Saint Joseph is the most loving of fathers. Saint Joseph is always ready to listen to you, always attentive, always understanding.

> If discouragement overwhelms you, think of the faith of Joseph;
>
> If anxiety has its grip on you, think of the hope of Joseph;
>
> If exasperation or hatred seizes you, think of the love of Joseph, who was the first man to set eyes on the human face of God in the person of the Infant conceived by the Holy Spirit in the womb of the Virgin Mary. Let us praise and thank Christ for having drawn so close to us, and for giving us Joseph as an example and model of love.[3]
>
> — Pope Benedict XVI

Discussion Questions:
1. What are the Corporal Works of Mercy? And how can you remember them?
2. Is suffering always a bad thing? How can St. Joseph, the loving father, comfort you when you are suffering?
3. Have you ever felt overwhelmed or anxious or seized by hatred? How can St. Joseph help you in these times?

Daily Prayers to Recite: Pray the Litany of St. Joseph (found on page 15) and the "Prayer Taught to the Children at Fatima" (found on page 18).

DAY 29

Hope of the Sick, *Pray for Us*

God loves to heal people through the intercession of St. Joseph! This includes healings of both St. Teresa of Avila and St. Thérèse of Lisieux.

Saint Teresa of Avila was once so sick that she thought she was dying. After prayers to St. Joseph, she was cured miraculously.

Saint Thérèse of Lisieux would have died as a baby, if not for St. Joseph's help. Saint Thérèse's parents, Saints Louis and Zélie Martin, were very devoted to St. Joseph.

Another Holy Family, Saints Zélie, Thérèse, and Louis Martin.

Saints Louis and Zélie named two of their children after Joseph, but both of these babies died in childbirth. St. Zélie thought her next baby was going to be a boy, and she planned to name the baby Joseph again. But the baby was a girl. They named her "Thérèse."

Soon after her birth, Thérèse became very, very sick. No one knew why baby Thérèse was sick. Zélie feared that Thérèse was going to die like her last two babies. Zélie knelt before a statue of St. Joseph in her bedroom and asked that he would heal Thérèse. Suddenly and miraculously, Thérèse was healed!

Zélie wrote the following about Thérèse's miracle:

> I went up to my room [little Thérèse was on the first
> floor with a wet nurse]. I knelt at the feet of St. Joseph.
> I asked him for the grace of healing for the little one,
> while resigning myself to God's will. I do not often cry,
> but I was crying as I prayed. I didn't know if I should
> go downstairs. In the end, I decided to go down, and
> what did I see?

> The baby was nursing vigorously. She did not let go
> until 1 p.m. She spit up a bit and fell back as though
> dead on her wet nurse. There were five of us around her.
> Everyone was stunned.

> Then, there was a worker who was crying. I felt my blood
> run cold. It looked like the baby was not breathing. It
> did no good for us to lean over to try and discover a
> sign of life because we could see nothing. But [baby
> Thérèse] was so calm, so peaceful, that I thanked God
> for having her die so gently.

> Then, a quarter of an hour went by, and my little
> Thérèse opened her eyes and started to smile.[1]

Isn't that an incredible story? Saint Zélie prayed for St.
Joseph's help even though she was sure her daughter was
going to die. Then, suddenly, the baby was nursing.

Then, they thought the baby had died all over again.
Instead of growing angry, St. Zélie thanked God for giving
her baby a gentle death. And again, the baby was alive. The
future St. Thérèse was smiling up at her parents.

SAINT JOSEPH OFFERS HOPE IN TIMES OF SICKNESS. Do you
know somebody who is sick? Go to St. Joseph! Saint Joseph
is your spiritual father. He wants you to go to him for help
and healing.

It's up to God whether somebody will be healed phys-
ically, but it is important to always ask for help. This is what
St. Zélie did for St. Thérèse. Zélie had asked for healing many

times before for her two babies that died. Even though she thought Thérèse was also going to die, she still went to St. Joseph and asked for help. And it worked. Thérèse was miraculously healed.

Remember, though: even if you are healed, you will still suffer in life. Saint Thérèse was healed as a baby, but she still suffered sickness in life. She was sick a lot in her life, but this suffering helped make her a saint.

How can suffering help us become saints? Saint Thérèse embraced her suffering out of love for Jesus. She wanted to be close to Jesus, who suffered terribly on the Cross. In her suffering, Thérèse came very close to Jesus.

Do you see how God can bless us in sickness and in health? Saint Joseph vowed to be faithful to his wife, Mary, in sickness and in health. Go to Joseph in sickness and in health, and he will help you. Saint Joseph will help you count your blessings in sickness and in health. He will help you abandon yourself to God's will for your life.

Discussion Questions:
1. Why did St. Zélie pray for St. Joseph's help even though she was sure that her daughter was going to die? Why is it important to pray even when our hope falters?
2. How can suffering help you to become a saint? How did St. Thérèse embrace her suffering? How did St. Joseph embrace his suffering?

Daily Prayers to Recite: Pray the Litany of St. Joseph (found on page 15) and the "Prayer Taught to the Children at Fatima" (found on page 18).

DAY 30
Patron of the Dying, *Pray for Us*

The name of Joseph will be our protection during all the days of our life, but above all at the moment of death.[1]

— Blessed William Joseph Chaminade

Saint Joseph died a holy and happy death. Why was St. Joseph's death so holy and so happy – can you guess why? Saint Joseph died in the arms of both Jesus and Mary. Can you think of a more beautiful way to die?

We entrust ourselves to St. Joseph, so that we, too, will experience a holy and happy death.

Do you know the story of *The Little Match Girl*?[2] It is a Hans Christian Anderson fairy tale, but — let me warn you — it's a sad story.

It's the story of a nameless girl who is afraid to go home on New Year's Eve. Her family is very poor. She helps feed her family by selling matchsticks, but she didn't sell any this day. Everybody she met in the street brushed her away or ignored her.

The little match girl is afraid to go home. She knows her dad will be very angry with her and might even hit her, because she didn't sell any matchsticks.

It is also very cold. The little match girl is barefoot in the snow and freezing. She huddles in an alleyway to get out of the cold, cold wind.

She lights a match for the little bit of warmth it gives off as it burns. She keeps lighting the matches, one by one. Each time, the light of the match shows her something beautiful: a warm stove, a holiday feast, a happy family, and a Christmas tree.

But each time, the beautiful image fades as the matchstick burns out.

In the cold night sky, the little match girl sees a shooting star. She remembers what her grandmother told her about shooting stars. A shooting star means a soul is going to Heaven.

The Little Match Girl's last match

In the flame of the next match, the little match girl sees her grandmother. Her grandmother was the only person in the world who had ever treated her kindly.

The little match girl cannot bear to see her grandmother fade away, too. Immediately, she lights all the matches.

When the flames of all burning matches finally burn away, the little match girl has died. Her grandmother has carried her away to Heaven. The shooting star she had seen in the sky had been her own soul going to Heaven.

The next morning, the little match girl is found in the alleyway. Everybody is very sad about her death. They do not know about her beautiful visions. They do not know that her grandmother has carried her away to Heaven.

SAINT JOSEPH WILL HELP CARRY YOU TO HEAVEN. Just like the little match girl's grandmother, St. Joseph will help guide you and carry you to Heaven. Getting to Heaven is a journey. St. Joseph will be your guide and protector on the journey to Heaven, just like St. Joseph was Jesus and Mary's guide and protector on their journey to Bethlehem, to Egypt, and back home to Nazareth.

The journey to Heaven can be especially dangerous when someone is nearing death:

> Jesus granted to [St. Joseph] the special privilege of safeguarding the dying against the snares of Lucifer, just as [St. Joseph] had also saved [Jesus] from the schemes of Herod.[3]
>
> — St. Alphonsus Liguori

With St. Joseph at your side in life and in death, you do not need to fear death.

Pray, also, that St. Joseph will be with your loved ones when they die. Saint Joseph will also console and protect those left behind when somebody dies.

Death is a really hard part of life, but St. Joseph helps ease the pain, even as Jesus takes away the sting of death.

The *Catechism* tells us to prepare for death by "entrust[ing] ourselves to St. Joseph."[4] Consecrate yourself to Jesus through St. Joseph, live a holy life, and you have nothing to fear about death.

Discussion Questions:
1. What was the shooting star that the little match girl saw? How was the little match girl comforted during her death?
2. Should you fear death?
3. Who will guide us and help carry us to Heaven?

Daily Prayers to Recite: Pray the Litany of St. Joseph (found on page 15) and the "Prayer Taught to the Children at Fatima" (found on page 18).

DAY 31

Terror of Demons, *Pray for Us*

Demons fear Jesus. Demons fear Mary. Did you know that demons fear St. Joseph as well? Demons are terrified when you ask St. Joseph for help — they are filled with terror.

Why are demons so terrified of St. Joseph? He is the husband of Mary and the father of Jesus. Saint Joseph saved our Savior from King Herod. Saint Joseph spent decades in adoration. St. Joseph's "yes" to God made it possible for Jesus to sacrifice Himself on Mt. Calvary, and that sacrifice crushed Satan and all demons forever.

Demons have plenty to fear from St. Joseph. He is mighty!

SAINT JOSEPH IS A DRAGON SLAYER! "Terror of Demons" is the title of a warrior. Saint Joseph wields a mighty spiritual weapon: the sword of purity. Saint Joseph's sword destroys dragons, monsters, and all the forces of darkness.

Do you remember Peter from *The Lion, the Witch, and the Wardrobe*? The evil White Witch, who is like Satan, is terrified when she hears that Peter and his brother and sisters have come to Narnia. The White Witch knows her terrible reign of "always winter, never Christmas" is coming to an end.

And speaking of Christmas, do you remember what gift Father Christmas gives to Peter? A mighty sword.

The evil White Witch sends wolves to attack Peter's sisters. This is like the Devil sending demons to attack us. Do you remember what Peter did?

Peter drew his sword and slayed the leader of the wolves. Aslan gave him the title "wolfsbane." From then on, Peter and his sword struck fear and terror in the hearts of the wolves and all of the White Witch's evil creatures.

Saint Joseph is like Peter Wolfsbane. Saint Joseph and his sword of purity strike terror in the hearts of the demons. Let him fight for you.

King Peter of Narnia

SAINT JOSEPH WILL PROTECT YOU AGAINST SATAN AND HIS DEMONS. Satan is not a myth. He is real. The world thinks Satan and his demons are just fairy tales and legends. They are not. Satan and his demons are constantly attacking us and our world.

Speaking of Peter of Narnia, here is how St. Peter the Apostle and first pope described the devil and the danger he causes:

> ... The devil is prowling around like a roaring lion looking for someone to devour. Resist him, steadfast in your faith, knowing that your fellow believers through-out the world undergo the same sufferings.

> — 1 Peter 5:8-9

To defeat the devil, you need Jesus, Mary, St. Joseph, and the teachings and Sacraments of the Catholic Church. Every Christian needs the sword of St. Joseph fighting for them. Go to Joseph when you need help fighting off demons and Satan's attacks.

Saint Joseph is your father, like he was Jesus' father. Run to your spiritual father for help, just like Jesus did. St. Joseph will fight for you. The Terror of Demons, St. Joseph Dragonsbane, is ready to slay dragons for you!

Discussion Questions:
1. Why was Peter given the title "Wolfsbane"? Why would St. Joseph be called "Dragonsbane"?
2. Who and what sword strike fear in the heart of the demons?
3. How can you defeat the devil?

Daily Prayers to Recite: Pray the Litany of St. Joseph (found on page 15) and the "Prayer Taught to the Children at Fatima" (found on page 18).

DAY 32

Protector of the Holy Church, *Pray for Us*

The Church needs the protection of St. Joseph. Saint Pope Paul VI tells us that Christ entrusted to St. Joseph "the care and protection of his own frail childhood."[1] Even from Heaven, St. Joseph continues to protect the "always weak, always under attack" Body of Jesus, which is the Church.[2]

The Church has been under constant attack since its birth at the Cross, like the Holy Family was under attack since Jesus' birth at Bethlehem. From the beginning and even now, the Church has been attacked from the inside and the outside. Judas, Jesus' own apostle, attacked the unborn Church and betrayed Jesus. Saul of Tarsus was a cruel attacker of the Church — he called for the stoning of St. Stephen — until Jesus called him. Saul converted and became St. Paul.

Many people have fallen away from the Church because of these attacks on and from within the Church. We need St. Joseph to protect the Church from outside attacks. We also need St. Joseph to direct the Church toward safety, unity, and truth, as he did the Holy Family.

Wolves are always attacking the Church, for all time, from the inside and from the outside. We need St. Joseph to protect the Church.

Do you remember the story of *Old Yeller*?[3] Old Yeller was the beloved, faithful, and "dingy yellow" dog of young Travis Coates. Calling somebody "yellow" is calling them a coward, but Old Yeller was no coward.

Old Yeller was originally a stray dog and unwelcome visitor to the Coates family ranch, while Travis' dad was away on a cattle drive. Travis hates Old Yeller and calls him a "rascal," but grows to love him.

Old Yeller rescues the family again and again. Old Yeller saves Travis' dad from a bear and Travis, himself, from a pack of wild hogs.

Travis with his faithful dog, Old Yeller

Towards the end of the story, Travis and his family are attacked by a wolf. Not just any wolf, this wolf was rabid. Rabid means the wolf had a disease that affected its brain and made the wolf crazy. One bite from this wolf, and Old Yeller would slowly become rabid, too, and eventually die a terrible death.

All by himself, Old Yeller protects the family from the wolf. Even though one bite would give him rabies, Old Yeller endured many bites. Old Yeller laid down his life for his family.

This is what St. Joseph does for the Church. Saint Joseph is the faithful watchdog and protector of the Church.

The wolves that attack the Church are also rabid and crazy. The wolves rarely understand what they are attacking when they attack the Church. The Church is truth and beauty, but in their madness, the wolves only see red.

Saint Joseph will endure many bites from the rabid wolves, like Old Yeller did. Unlike Old Yeller, St. Joseph will never be infected by the wolves' lies and never lose sight of Truth.

SAINT JOSEPH PROTECTS THE CHURCH. Saint Joseph will help the Church in times of persecution and attack.

Miguel Pro, a young priest, lived during a time when the Catholic Church was under terrible attack in his home country of Mexico. Father Miguel loved St. Joseph. He said his first Mass at an altar of St. Joseph. So, when Father Miguel and his church were attacked, he turned to St. Joseph for help.

Saint Joseph gave Father Miguel great strength and courage. Father Miguel gave up his life as a martyr for Christ. Father Miguel stood bravely before the firing squad with his arms stretched out like Jesus, crucifix in one hand, rosary in the other, and St. Joseph in his heart. His death changed the hearts of the Church's persecutors forever. Father Miguel shouted "Viva Cristo Rey!" or "Long live Christ the King!" His words inspired the firing squad, who refused to shoot him — all but one. Father Miguel's words inspired the rest of his country, too, to fight for the Church.

Father Miguel Pro is now known as Blessed Miguel Pro, and his words echo even now, "Viva Cristo Rey!"

Like Blessed Miguel Pro, hold fast to Jesus, Mary, and St. Joseph. They are with us always.

Lamb of God, who takes away the sins of the world,
Spare us, O Lord.

Lamb of God, who takes away the sins of the world,
Graciously hear us, O Lord.

Lamb of God, who takes away the sins of the world,
Have mercy on us.

Discussion Questions:
1. What did Old Yeller do to protect Travis and his family?
2. Who is the faithful watchdog and protector of the Church?
3. Who or what is attacking the Church? And how does St. Joseph protect us from these enemies?

Daily Prayers to Recite: Pray the Litany of St. Joseph (found on page 15) and the "Prayer Taught to the Children at Fatima" (found on page 18).

DAY 33

He Made Him the Lord of His Household, And Prince Over All His Possessions

> As Almighty God appointed Joseph, son of the patriarch Jacob, over all the land of Egypt to save grain for the people, so [also] when the fullness of time was come and God was about to send on earth His only-begotten Son, the Savior of the world, God chose another Joseph of whom the first had been a type, and God made [St. Joseph] the lord and chief of his household and possessions, the guardian of God's choicest treasures.[1]
>
> — Blessed Pope Pius IX

Our spiritual father is St. Joseph, and St. Joseph is the lord, chief, and guardian of the treasures of heaven. That is a huge statement. Your spiritual father is a wealthier man than any king in history or any billionaire in the world.

Do you remember the musical *Annie*? Annie is a poor orphan living in a poor, rundown orphanage. The orphans sing "It's the Hard Knock Life" about their lives, saying, "No one cares for you a smidge, when you're in an orphanage."[2] She is chosen to come to live with an extremely rich man named Oliver Warbucks. Annie eventually melts the heart of Warbucks, and he adopts Annie.

Annie goes from rags to riches when she is adopted, but Warbucks' wealth is nothing compared to the treasures of Heaven, of which your adopted father, St. Joseph, is lord and guardian.

SAINT JOSEPH WANTS TO SHARE THE GREATEST TREASURES WITH YOU. Saint Joseph is not a miser like Daddy Warbucks or Ebenezer Scrooge who wants to keep all the treasures for himself. Saint Joseph wants to share all this with you as your spiritual father.

Remember, again, *Willy Wonka and the Chocolate Factory*. Do you remember why Willy Wonka sends out all the golden tickets?

Illustration from *Charlie and the Chocolate Factory*

Finders of the golden tickets seemed to be promised a lifetime supply of chocolate. The golden tickets themselves didn't quite say this. Instead, the following was written on the tickets:

> Greetings to you, the lucky finder of this Golden Ticket, from Mr. Willy Wonka! I shake you warmly by the hand! Tremendous things are in store for you! Many wonderful surprises await you! For now, I do invite you to come to my factory and be my guest for one whole day ... when it is time to leave, you will be escorted home by a procession of large trucks. These trucks, I can tell you are good, you will be loaded with enough delicious eatables to last you and your entire household for many years ... In your wildest dreams, you could not imagine such things could happen to you![3]

A lifetime supply of chocolate would be a great treasure, right? For some boys and girls, like those in the *Willy Wonka* book and movie, it was the greatest treasure they could ever possibly imagine.

But what was the real reason Willy Wonka sent out those golden tickets?

Willy Wonka had no children of his own, but he needed someone to take over and care for his chocolate factory when he was gone. Willy Wonka could not sell his chocolate factory to greedy rival candy makers like Arthur Slugworth. Willy Wonka also could not leave his chocolate factory to just any child. Children could be greedy and vicious, like Augustus Gloop and Violet Beauregarde. Willy Wonka needed somebody to care for his oompa-loompas, not boss them around, like Veruca Salt.

Willy Wonka needed to find a kind, loving, and virtuous boy, like Charlie Bucket to take over his chocolate factory and become "lord over all his possessions."

Like the virtuous Charlie Bucket, St. Joseph lovingly protects and cares for the world's greatest treasures, Jesus and Mary. St. Joseph will also increase the virtues in you. St. Joseph will share with you the treasures of heaven, so your vices don't destroy you, like they destroyed the other children who found golden tickets.

Seated beside Jesus in the Kingdom of Heaven, St. Joseph wants to give you far greater treasures than chocolate and golden tickets.

Saint Joseph will equip you with the sword of purity, which is greater even than the sword of King Peter of Narnia.

Saint Joseph will increase your courage greater even than Old Yeller, Prince Philip of *Sleeping Beauty*, and St. George.

Saint Joseph Most Just, Most Chaste, Most Prudent, Most Courageous, Most Obedient, and Most Faithful will adorn you with the most beautiful and richest jewels in the world: the virtues.

And St. Joseph will share with you the greatest of all treasures, Jesus and Mary. Consecrate yourself to St. Joseph, so he will increase your intimacy with Jesus and Mary.

Discussion Questions:
1. What is the grand prize that Willy Wonka gives Charlie Bucket?
2. What are the treasures of the Church that St. Joseph can share with you?

Continue to the next section, "Day of Consecration."

Day of Consecration

O God, who, in your loving providence, chose Blessed Joseph to be the spouse of your most Holy Mother, grant us the favor of having him for our intercessor in heaven whom on earth we venerate as our protector. You, who love and reign forever and ever. Amen.

Today is the day! You did it. Today, you are going to consecrate yourself to St. Joseph. It's a big day. Your life will start to change today. One day, you will look back and say this day was a turning point.

Never before in the history of the Church have we had a comprehensive Consecration to St. Joseph. Many saints have sought to honor St. Joseph and love him with devotions, but this is something bigger than before. This is a new era of devotion to St. Joseph. You are among the very first in the history of the Church to share in it.

We are here at the beginning of the era of St. Joseph!

He will defend our families against the new attacks on the family, the likes of which we have never seen before.

The Holy Trinity wants St. Joseph to be more known and loved. You have been invited to imitate the virtues and holiness of St. Joseph's pure heart. With St. Joseph's help, virtues and holiness will increase in your life. With St. Joseph's paternal cloak wrapped around you, you will be protected from spiritual harm.

Fear nothing, my friend. All the armies of the earth and hell below could not overcome the simple craftsman and carpenter from Nazareth, whom God chose to protect the Holy Family. Neither will you be overcome. Your spiritual father is the father of Jesus, the husband of the Mother of God, and the Terror of Demons!

HONOR YOUR SPIRITUAL FATHER. For the rest of your life, love, trust, and honor St. Joseph.

Those who honor their father atone for sins ... In word and deed, honor your father, that all blessings may come to you.

— Sirach 3:3, 8

Go to St. Joseph in good times and bad, plenty and poverty, health and sickness. Saint Joseph will be your guardian, your strength, and your guide. You will never be lost following St. Joseph.

Go to St. Joseph. If you become tired, go to Joseph. If you become scared, go to Joseph. If you are alone, mourning, or tempted, RUN to Joseph!

Saint Joseph will never be far from you. He will hear your voice, and he will fly to your aid. Saint Joseph will be your instant defense. Saint Joseph, a fearless warrior and your spiritual father, will rush to your side with his sword raised. He will protect you, always.

God demands much from you, but He will favor you generously on this earth, and will exalt you, if you but imitate St. Joseph in his virtues.[1]

— St. Joseph Sebastian Pelczar

Never forget what you have learned while preparing for this consecration. Renew your consecration often, even daily.

Strive to please the loving heart of your spiritual father. Avoid sin. Live as a faithful member of the Church. If you continue to struggle with sin or a particularly stubborn sin, get back up again. Go to Joseph. Keep your eyes fixed on Jesus, Mary, and St. Joseph.

Jesus, Mary, and St. Joseph will never disappoint you. They will never abandon you. They will always love you and be with you.

I have prayed to our Lord that he might give me St. Joseph for a father, as he had given me Mary for a mother. I have prayed that the Lord might put in my heart that devotion, that confidence, that child-like love of a ... devotee of St. Joseph. I trust the good Master has heard my prayers, for I now feel greater devotion to this great saint, and I am full of confidence and hope.[2]

— St. Peter Julian Eymard

Pray the Children's Act of Consecration to St. Joseph on the following page.

If you are consecrating your family to St. Joseph, pray the Family Act of Consecration to St. Joseph (found on page 144).

Children's Act of Consecration to St. Joseph[3]

I, _____, a child of God, take you, St. Joseph, to be my spiritual father. I know that Jesus and Mary have brought me to you. Jesus and Mary want me to know you, to love you, and to be totally consecrated to you, St. Joseph, my father forever.

I have spent many days coming to know and love you better. Now, I consecrate myself to you, St. Joseph. I want you in my life more and more. I need you in my life. Take me as your spiritual child, O great St. Joseph! Please take all that I am and give it to Jesus. I do not want to hold anything back.

As the husband of Mary, you provided for my spiritual mother. Thank you for always being faithful to her. Thank you for loving her. Thank you for giving your entire life to serving Mary and Jesus.

As the virginal father of Jesus, you cared for my Lord. You protected my Lord from evil men. Thank you for guarding the life of my Savior. Thanks to you, Jesus was able to sacrifice His life for me on the Cross. Thanks to you, St. Joseph, I can hope for everlasting life in Heaven.

As my spiritual father, I trust that you will guide and protect me, as you guided and protected Jesus and Mary. Please increase in me virtues and holiness and prayerfulness. I want to grow to be more and more like you, St. Joseph. I want to be pure, humble, loving, and merciful, like you.

Now that I am yours and you are mine, I promise never to forget you. I know you will never forget me. This gives me such great joy! I am loved by St. Joseph! I belong forever to St. Joseph!

Praise to the Holy Trinity — the Father, the Son, and the Holy Spirit — who has blessed you and raised you to be the greatest saint after the Virgin Mary.

Praise also to the Virgin Mary, who loves you and wants all the world to love you.

Praise to you, St. Joseph, my father, my guardian, my all! Amen.

Family Act of Consecration to St. Joseph

We, the _____ family, take you, St. Joseph, to be our spiritual father. We are confident that Jesus and Mary have led us to you; to know you, to love you, and to be totally consecrated to you.

Therefore, having come to know and love you, we consecrate our family entirely to you, St. Joseph. We want you in our lives; we need you in our lives. Take us as your spiritual children, O great St. Joseph! We desire to hold nothing back from your protective fatherhood.

As the husband of Mary, you provided for our spiritual mother. Thank you for always being faithful to her. Thank you for loving her and giving your entire life for her service.

As the virginal father of Jesus, you cared for our Lord and protected Him from evil men. Thank you for guarding the life of our Savior. Thanks to you, Jesus was able to shed His Blood for us on the Cross. Thanks to you, St. Joseph, we have hope of everlasting life in Heaven.

As our spiritual father, we know that you will guide and protect us, too. Please instruct us in the ways of prayer, virtue, and holiness. We want to be like you, St. Joseph. We want to be pure, humble, loving, and merciful.

Now that we are yours and you are ours, we promise never to forget you. We know that you will never forget us, and this gives us boundless joy! We are loved by St. Joseph! We belong to St. Joseph! Amen!

References

Introduction

[1] Servant of God Catherine Doherty, *Grace in Every Season: Through the Year with Catherine Doherty* (Combermere, Canada: Madonna House, 2001), 125.

Prayers

[1] Pope St. Pius X approved this prayer on November 26, 1906 invoking St. Joseph as the virgin father of Jesus. Pius X granted an indulgence to all who recite this prayer.

Days 1-7

[1] Genesis 3:15

Day 1

[1] For more on this, read *The Theology of Sci-Fi: The Christian's Guide to the Galaxy* by the same author, Scott L. Smith, Jr.

Day 2

[1] The version of the litany included in this book is the version approved by Pope St. Pius X ("the tenth") in 1909.
[2] St. Madeleine Sophie Barat, as quoted in Levy, *Joseph the Just Man*, 147-148.

Day 3

[1] Blessed William Joseph Chaminade, *Marian Writings*, vol. 1, ed. J.B. Armbruster, SM (Dayton, OH: Marianist Press, 1980), 223-224.

Days 8-15 Overview

[1] John 6:51
[2] Ibid.

Day 8

[1] Matthew 22:12

Day 9

[1] For more on this, read *The Lord of the Rings and the Eucharist* from the same author, Scott L. Smith, Jr.

Day 10

[1] Blessed William Joseph Chaminade, Marian Writings, vol. 1, ed. J. B. Armbruster, SM (Dayton, OH: Marianist Press, 1980), 230.

Day 11

[1] The following version of Sleeping Beauty is based on the Disney adaptation. Disney's version is based in part on the 1890 ballet *The Sleeping Beauty* by Pyotr Ilyich Tchaikovsky. In particular, the melody of Aurora's song "Once Upon a Dream" is based on the "Grande valse villageoise" (nicknamed "The Garland Waltz") from Tchaikovsky's ballet.

[2] From Act 1, scene 1 of Shakespeare's *A Midsummer Night's Dream*

Day 12

[1] St. Francis de Sales, as quoted in Francis L. Filas, SJ, Joseph and *Jesus: A Theological Study of Their Relationship* (Milwaukee, WI: Bruce Publishing Co., 1952), 99.

[2] Matthew 5:8, "The Beatitudes"

[3] Pride is Doc, Lust is Happy, Anger (wrath) is Grumpy, Greed is Dopey, Gluttony is Bashful, Envy is Sneezy, Sloth is Sleepy.

Day 14

[1] St. Josemaría Escrivá, Christ is Passing By (New York, NY: Scepter, 1973), 93.

[2] John 10:11

[3] Blessed William Joseph Chaminade, *The Chaminade Legacy*, vol. 2, Notes for Conferences and Sermons, trans. Joseph Stefanelli, SM (Dayton, OH: North American Center for Marianist Studies, 2008), 416.

Day 15

[1] St. Peter Julian Eymard, *Month of St. Joseph* (Cleveland, OH: Emmanuel Publications, 1948), 6-7.

[2] Ephesians 5:32

[3] St. John Paul II, *Homily at the Shrine of St. Joseph in Kalisz, Poland*, June 4, 1997.

Days 16-22 Overview

[1] Pride is defeated by Humility; Lust is defeated by Chastity; Anger is defeated by Patience; Greed is defeated by Generosity; Gluttony is defeated by Temperance; Envy is defeated by Charity; Sloth is defeated by Courage or Fortitude

Day 16

[1] Pope Pius XI, Encyclical Letter *Divini Redemptoris* (*On Atheistic Communism*), March 19, 1937, no. 81.

[2] The phrase was popularized by Cicero in *De Natura Deorum: iustitia suum cuique distribuit*, "justice renders to everyone his due."

This definition was later codified in Justinian's Code of Civil Law: "Justice is a habit whereby a man renders to each one his due with constant and perpetual will." The idea also traces back to Plato's Republic 4.433.

[3] cf. Genesis 7:1; 18:23-32: Ezekiel 18:5ff; Proverbs 12:10.

[4] cf. Tobit 7:6; 9:6.

[5] St. Josemaría Escrivá, *Christ is Passing By* (New York, NY: Scepter, 1973), 40.

[6] St. Francis de Sales, as quoted in Rosalie Marie Levy, *Joseph the Just Man* (Derby, NY: Daughters of St. Paul, 1955), 140.

Day 17

[1] Luke 12:34

[2] From the ecstasies of Saint Gemma recorded by members of the Giannini family in the summer of 1902, specifically on Monday, August 11, around 9:00am. *Estasi-Diario-Autobiografia-Scritti Vari di Santa Gemma Galgani.*

[3] Ibid.

Day 18

[1] *Catechism of the Catholic Church*, no. 1806.

[2] The Martyrologies of Tallagh, of Marianus O'Gorman, and of Donegal record that on St. Patrick's return from Munster, about the year 451 or 456 AD, the Irish Apostle entered Hy-Failge territory. The wicked pagan chieftain was named Failge Berraide and the full name of the Irish idol was "Crom Cruach." From *Lives of the Irish Saints by John*, Canon O'Hanlon (1821-1905).

Day 19

[1] From Jacobus da Varagine's *Legenda aurea* (*The Golden Legend*), ca. 1260

[2] John 16:33

Day 20

[1] St. Joseph Sebastian Pelczar, as quoted in the unpublished manuscript "Meditation 48: The Imitation of St. Joseph in the Interior Life," trans. Mother Agnieszka Kijowska, SSCJ. Courtesy of Sr. Mary Joseph Calore, SSCJ and Mother Klara Slonina, SSCJ.

[2] Genesis 3:1

[3] Pope Benedict XVI, as quoted in Fr. Richard W. Gilsdorf, *Go to Joseph* (Green Bay, WI: Star of the Bay Press, 2009), 122.

Day 21

[1] Hebrews 11:1.

[2] St. John Paul II, *Letter to Cardinal Angelo Sodano for the 6th International Symposium on St. Joseph*, August 21, 1993. English translation courtesy of Miss Ileana E. Salazar, MA.

Days 23-33 Overview

[1] St. John Paul II, Apostolic Exhortation *Redemptoris Custos* (*On the Person and Mission of St. Joseph in the Life of Christ and of the Church*), no. 8, available at www.vatican.va.

Day 23

[1] St. Francis de Sales, as quoted in Rosalie Marie Levy, *Joseph the Just Man* (Derby, NY: Daughters of St. Paul, 1955), 129-130.

[2] Matthew 2:11

[3] Leviticus 12:6-7

[4] Leviticus 12:8

[5] Matthew 5:3

Day 24

[1] St. John Paul II, Apostolic Exhortation *Redemptoris Custos* (*On the Person and Mission of St. Joseph in the Life of Christ and of the Church*), no. 22, available at www.vatican.va.

[2] Genesis 3:19

[3] Matthew 11:28-30

[4] 1996 study by Forrest N. Easley, a forester and wood technologist for the United States Forest Services and the United States Naval Research Laboratory.

[5] St. Peter Julian Eymard, *Month of St. Joseph* (Cleveland, OH: Emmanuel Publications, 1948), 2.

[6] Blessed William Joseph Chaminade, *Marian Writings*, vol. 1, ed. J.B. Armbruster, SM (Dayton, OH: Marianist Press, 1980), 235.

Day 25

[1] Luke 2:52

[2] St. Josemaría Escrivá, *Christ is Passing By* (New York, NY: Scepter, 1973), 119-121.

Day 26

[1] St. Thérèse of Lisieux, *Story of a Soul* (New York, NY: Image Books, 1957), 77.

Day 27

[1] Blessed Anne Catherine Emmerich, *The Complete Visions of Anne Catherine Emmerich* (San Bernardino, CA: Catholic Book Club, 2013), 127. Note to readers: The private revelations of Blessed Anne Catherine Emmerich, in which she claims to have seen or been present at certain events in the life of Jesus, Mary, and the saints, have not been authenticated by the Catholic Church. Most of Emmerich's mystical experiences were written down by her friend, the poet Clemens Brentano, and we cannot now know what was colored by Brentano's own ideas and poetic exaggerations. Nevertheless, the accounts do tell us the gist of what Emmerich experienced, though not accurate in every detail.

Day 28

[1] The seven Spiritual Works of Mercy are: Teach the Ignorant, Pray for the Living and the Dead, Correct Sinners, Counsel Those in Doubt, Console the Sorrowful, Bear Wrongs Patiently, and Forgive Wrongs Willingly.

[2] St. Joseph Marello, as quoted by the Oblates of St. Joseph. The website for the Shrine of St. Joseph, Guardian of the Redeemer, is located at https:// www.shrinestjoseph.com/.

[3] Pope Benedict XVI, *Address in Yaounde, Cameroon (March 19, 2009)*, as quoted in Jose A. Rodrigues, *The Book of Joseph: God's Chosen Father* (Toronto, ON: Ave Maria Centre of Peace, 2017), 119.

Day 29

[1] St. Zélie Martin, as quoted in Helene Mongin, *The Extraordinary Parents of St. Thérèse of Lisieux* (Huntington, IN: Our Sunday Visitor, 2015), 105-106. Quote modified by the author for ease of reading to children.

Day 30

[1] Blessed William Joseph Chaminade, as quoted in Maria Cecilia Baij, OSB, *The Life of St. Joseph* (Asbury, NJ: 101 Foundation, Inc., 1996), 421.

[2] In Danish, *Den Lille Pige med Svovlstikkerne*, meaning "the little girl with the matchsticks"; first published 1845.

[3] St. Alphonsus Liguori, as quoted in Maria Cecilia Baij, OSB, *The Life of St. Joseph* (Asbury, NJ: 101 Foundation, Inc., 1996), 416.

[4] *Catechism of the Catholic Church*, paragraph no. 1014.

Day 32

[1] St. Pope Paul VI, "Homily on the Solemnity of St. Joseph," March 19, 1969, as quoted in Jose A. Rodrigues, *The Book of Joseph: God's Chosen Father* (Toronto, ON: Ave Maria Centre of Peace, 2017), 120.

[2] Ibid.

[3] Gipson, Fred, *Old Yeller*, 1956; 1957 film adaptation by Walt Disney.

Day 33

[1] Blessed Pope Pius IX, Decree *Quemadmadum Deus (St. Joseph as the Patron of the Universal Church)*, December 8, 1870.

[2] *Annie* musical, 1977; "It's the Hard Knock Life," music by Charles Strouse, lyrics by Martin Charnin.

[3] Dahl, Roald, and Joseph Schindelman, *Charlie and the Chocolate Factory* (New York: Knopf, 1964).

Day of Consecration

[1] St. Joseph Sebastian Pelczar, as quoted in the unpublished manuscript *Meditation 48: The Imitation of St. Joseph in the Interior Life*, trans. Mother Agnieszka Kijowska, SSCJ. Courtesy of Sr. Mary Joseph Calore, SSCJ and Mother Klara Slonina, SSCJ.

[2] St. Peter Julian Eymard, as quoted in Rosalie Marie Levy, *Joseph the Just Man* (Derby, NY: Daughters of St. Paul, 1955), 150; modified by the author for a children's audience.

[3] Adapted from Father Donald Calloway's Act of Consecration to St. Joseph.

List of Illustrations

Day 1: St. Joseph, "The Increaser," by Fr. Chris Decker.

Day 2: Our Lady of Knock, by Fr. Chris Decker.

Day 3: Mary Lennox finds Colin sick in bed in *The Secret Garden*, by Fr. Chris Decker.

Day 4: Willy Wonka leading the children into the chocolate room, a "world of [his] imagination," by Fr. Chris Decker.

Day 5: Aslan and Jill Pole in *The Silver Chair*, by Fr. Chris Decker.

Day 6: Scrooge and Tiny Tim, illustration from *A Christmas Carol*, by Fr. Chris Decker.

Day 7: A Queen Knighting a Soldier, by Fr. Chris Decker.

Day 8: Crane, Walter. "Cinderella's Fairy Godmother." 1897, University of Florida, George A. Smathers Libraries. Public domain.

Day 9: "When Adam's flesh and Adam's bone, sits at Cair Paravel in throne," by Scott L. Smith, Jr.

Day 10: Olympic torch bearer by Scott L. Smith, Jr.

Day 11: The shield of virtue defends against the fire-breathing dragon, by Scott L. Smith, Jr.

Day 12: Artist unknown. *Europa's Fairy Book*. "Snow White's Evil Queen." 1916, p. 201. Public domain.

Day 13: Anne of Green Gables illustration, Matthew presents Anne to Marilla, by Fr. Chris Decker.

Day 14: Father and Son: Merlin and Nemo, by Scott L. Smith, Jr.

Day 15: Lion King, Mufasa and Simba overlooking their kingdom, by Scott L. Smith, Jr.

Day 16: Little Red Hen baking bread, by Scott L. Smith, Jr.

Day 17: Artist unknown. "St. Dominic Savio." Public domain. Artist unknown. Public domain. "St. Gemma Galgani."

Day 18: Von Wagner, Alexander. "The Chariot Race." Manchester Art Gallery, web address: https://artuk.org/discover/artworks/the-chariot-race-206325

Artist unknown. "Ancient Irish Chariots on base of Cross of Clonmacnoise." *Wood-Martin's Pagan Ireland*. 9th century, Library Ireland, web address: https://www.libraryireland.com/Social-HistoryAncientIreland/III-XXIV-2.php

Day 19: St. George and the Dragon, by Fr. Chris Decker.

Day 20: Abraham is asked to sacrifice his child Isaac, by Scott L. Smith, Jr.

Day 21: Horton searching through the field of clover, by Scott L. Smith, Jr.

Day 22: Artist unknown. "St. Dominic Savio." Public domain.

Day 23: Smith, Essie Willcox. "They All Drew Near to the Fire" from *Little Women*. 1922. Public domain.

Day 24: Artist unknown. "The Miraculous Loretto Staircase, Santa Fe, New Mexico." Public domain.

Day 25: "St. Joseph, Custodian of the Two Hearts," by Norman Faucheux (2020).

Day 26: Dalmatian puppies, by Scott L. Smith, Jr.

Day 27: Columns on the facade of a building, by Scott L. Smith, Jr.

Day 28: St. Joseph, the Increaser, by Fr. Chris Decker.

Day 29: Another Holy Family, Saints Zélie, Thérèse, and Louis Martin. Artists unknown. Public domain.

Day 30: The Little Matchgirl's last match, by Scott L. Smith, Jr.

Day 31: King Peter of Narnia by Scott L. Smith, Jr.

Day 32: Travis with his faithful dog, Old Yeller, by Scott L. Smith, Jr.

Day 33: Illustration from *Charlie and the Chocolate Factory*, by Fr. Chris Decker.

Commissioned by Fr. Donald Calloway, MIC

St. Joseph, Terror of Demons
Y100-DD10GW

St. Joseph, Terror of Demons
Y100-WC10GW

St. Joseph, Terror of Demons
Y100-TE10GW

The Immaculata and the Terror of Demons
Y100-IM10GW

MARIAN INSPIRATION FROM FR. CALLOWAY

Consecration to St. Joseph:
The Wonders of Our Spiritual Father

In the midst of crisis, confusion, and a world at war with the Church, it's time to come home again to our spiritual father, St. Joseph. In this richly researched and lovingly presented program of consecration to St. Joseph, Fr. Calloway brings to life the wonders, the power, and the ceaseless love of St. Joseph, Patron of the Universal Church and the Terror of Demons. Paperback, 320 pages. Y100-FCSJ [e]
Also available in Spanish: Y100-SCSJ

Consecration to St. Joseph:
The Wonders of Our Spiritual Father –
Commemorative Edition

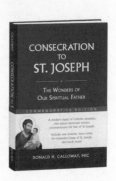

An expanded, premium hardcover edition of *Consecration to St. Joseph* includes a new foreword, 3 ribbons for marking pages, papal additions to the Litany of St. Joseph, more quotes from saints and blesseds about St. Joseph, Fr. Calloway's letter to the pope requesting a Year of St. Joseph, full-color artwork, and lots of other special new material. This will definitely be a keepsake to treasure! Hardcover, 368 pages. Y100-HCJO

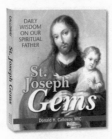

St. Joseph Gems:
Daily Wisdom on Our Spiritual Father

Father Calloway has gathered the largest collection of quotes about St. Joseph to ever appear in print. Selected from the writings of popes, saints, blesseds, and the many venerables of the Church, these quotes will help you rediscover the second-greatest saint in the Church, after the Blessed Virgin Mary! Paperback, 245 pages. Y100-SJEM

No Turning Back
A Witness to Mercy, 10th Anniversary Edition

In this 10th anniversary edition, Fr. Calloway looks back on the past decade in a new introduction to this perennially powerful witness to the transforming grace of God and the Blessed Mother's love for her children. His witness proves a key truth of our faith: Between Jesus, the Divine Mercy, and Mary, the Mother of Mercy, there's no reason to give up hope on anyone, no matter how far they are from God. Paperback, 288 pages. Includes photo section. Y100-ANTBK [e]

Call 1-800-462-7426 or visit fathercalloway.com

MARIAN INSPIRATION FROM FR. CALLOWAY

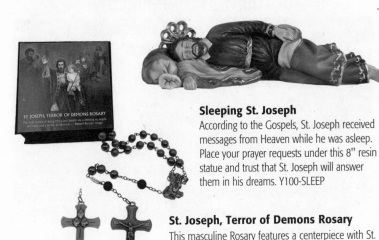

Sleeping St. Joseph

According to the Gospels, St. Joseph received messages from Heaven while he was asleep. Place your prayer requests under this 8" resin statue and trust that St. Joseph will answer them in his dreams. Y100-SLEEP

St. Joseph, Terror of Demons Rosary

This masculine Rosary features a centerpiece with St. Joseph on one side and Mary on the other, genuine hematite beads, and measures 25" long. Y100-SJTR

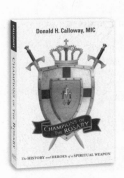

Champions of the Rosary: The History and Heroes of a Spiritual Weapon

Champions of the Rosary tells the powerful story of the history of the Rosary and the champions of this devotion. The Rosary is a spiritual sword with the power to conquer sin, defeat evil, and bring about peace. Read this book to deepen your understanding and love for praying the Rosary. Endorsed by 30 bishops from around the world! Paperback, 436 pages. Includes photo section. Y100-CRBK ℮

The Rosary: Spiritual Sword of Our Lady DVD

Father Donald Calloway, MIC, best-selling author of *Champions of the Rosary: The History and Heroes of a Spiritual Weapon*, explains the power of Our Lady's favorite devotion, the Rosary, in this engaging DVD. 1 hour, 53 minutes. Y100-RDVD

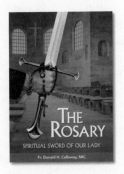

Call 1-800-462-7426 or visit fathercalloway.com

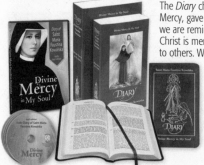

Join the
Association of Marian Helpers,
headquartered at the
National Shrine of The Divine Mercy,
and share in special blessings!

An invitation from
Fr. Joseph, MIC, director

Marian Helpers is an Association of Christian faithful of the Congregation of Marian Fathers of the Immaculate Conception. By becoming a member, you share in the spiritual benefits of the daily Masses, prayers, and good works of the Marian priests and brothers.

This is a special offer of grace given to you by the Church through the Marian Fathers. Please consider this opportunity to share in these blessings, along with others whom you would wish to join into this spiritual communion.

1-800-462-7426 • marian.org/join

Spiritual Enrollments & Masses

Enroll your loved ones in the Association of Marian Helpers, and they will participate in the graces from the daily Masses, prayers, good works, and merits of the Marian priests and brothers around the world.

Request a Mass to be offered by the Marian Fathers for your loved ones

Individual Masses
(for the living or deceased)

Gregorian Masses
(30 days of consecutive Masses for the deceased)

1-800-462-7426 • marian.org/enrollments • marian.org/mass